HERBERT MOLDERINGS

Marcel Duchamp at the Age of 85

Translated by John Brogden

With a text by Frederick Kiesler.

Published in collaboration with the Austrian Frederick and Lillian Kiesler Private Foundation, Vienna

HERBERT MOLDERINGS

Marcel Duchamp at the Age of 85

An Incunabulum of Conceptual Photography

Verlag der Buchhandlung Walther König
Köln 2013

Contents

Foreword

Archives are treasure troves of surprises. The most exciting of documents often remain hidden for years before their moment of glory – their discovery, their academic treatment, their publication – finally comes. One such archive is that of the Frederick and Lillian Kiesler Private Foundation, which was established in Vienna in 1997. The acquisition of Frederick Kiesler's estate, its transport from New York to Vienna and its public access within the scope of a foundation had been made possible through the generous help of the Republic of Austria, the Municipality of Vienna and private patrons. Taking many years, the perusal and processing of thousands of drawings, plans and photographs as well as a cornucopia of texts and correspondence brought forth a great many new and exciting finds and findings. Among the biggest surprises was a typescript laconically titled "I was waiting for Marcel – it was 5.35 p.m. at 42 West 57 Str., January 13, 1945". In this document, Frederick Kiesler, the Austro-American architect, designer, artist, stage designer and theoretician, describes with painstaking attention to detail the production of a portrait photograph of "Marcel Duchamp at the Age of 85" in the studio of a New York photographer. The euphoria triggered by this discovery was naturally closely bound up with questions concerning its possible academic treatment and first-ever publication. Herbert Molderings, an outstanding Duchamp researcher and photography historian, obligingly took up this exciting challenge. Kiesler's typescript turned out to be the key to the hitherto unsolved enigma posed by the photograph of Marcel Duchamp published in the magazine *View* in 1945.

Molderings' findings not only accord this famous portrait photograph of Marcel Duchamp its proper place in the artist's œuvre but also raise further questions that are worthy of consideration: questions concerning, for example, the reasons why Kiesler/Duchamp decided on the use of an objective, emotionless style for a description of the happenings in the photographer's studio manifesting the utmost attention to technical detail, such that the account of the process of producing the portrait seems to capture the scene with the precision of a short film sequence. Constituting an equally fascinating subject for research are the historically relevant points of contact in both the practical and the theoretical work of these two artists, whose ways of thinking and acting, despite their differences, both transcended existing conventions. Also worthy of particular attention in this connection is the personal relationship between Stefi and Frederick Kiesler and Marcel Duchamp. Just as sober as the title "I was waiting for Marcel ...", though operating on a completely different level, is the entry in Stefi Kiesler's desk diary of October 2, 1942: "cleaned Marcel's room". This terse note marked the beginning of the Kieslers' life with their lodger Marcel Duchamp in their New York penthouse (56, 7th Avenue), a period of cohabitation that was to last until October 1943. The intense personal relationship between these three friends, who had already got to know one another in Paris during the 1920s, continued until 1948, when it came to an end that was as abrupt as it was mysterious. The entries in Stefi's diary, which cover the period from the beginning of the 1930s until well into the late 1950s, mainly concern appointments and get-togethers with the Kieslers' friends and acquaintances: they are a veritable "Who's Who" of the New York art scene, complete with the dates and, often, the places of their meetings with individuals and groups. It was in this milieu, populated largely by exiled European artists, that Stefi Kiesler was able to function as an important mediator between artistic activities in Europe and the United States, not least by reason of her post in the Foreign Languages Department of the New York Public Library.

Between 1933 and 1951, Stefi noted the name of their friend Marcel Duchamp in her diaries as many as 122 times (17 times in 1942, 15 times each in 1943 and 1945, and 45 times in 1947, the year of Kiesler's and Duchamp's collaboration on the international exhibition "Le Surréalisme en 1947" at Galerie Maeght in Paris). At first she referred to him as "Marcel Duchamp", but then more and more frequently simply as "Duchamp" and latterly just by his forename "Marcel". This circumstance is worthy of special mention inasmuch as Stefi Kiesler referred to only a very few of their common friends by their forenames in her diary, this being a sign of particularly close friendship.

The Frederick and Lillian Kiesler Private Foundation is most indebted to Herbert Molderings both for his erudite treatment and publication of Frederick Kiesler's typescript, which has shed new light on the œuvre of Marcel Duchamp, and for the impulse his study has given for the further evaluation of this find at the archive of the Kiesler Foundation.

DIETER BOGNER
Austrian Frederick and Lillian Kiesler Private Foundation

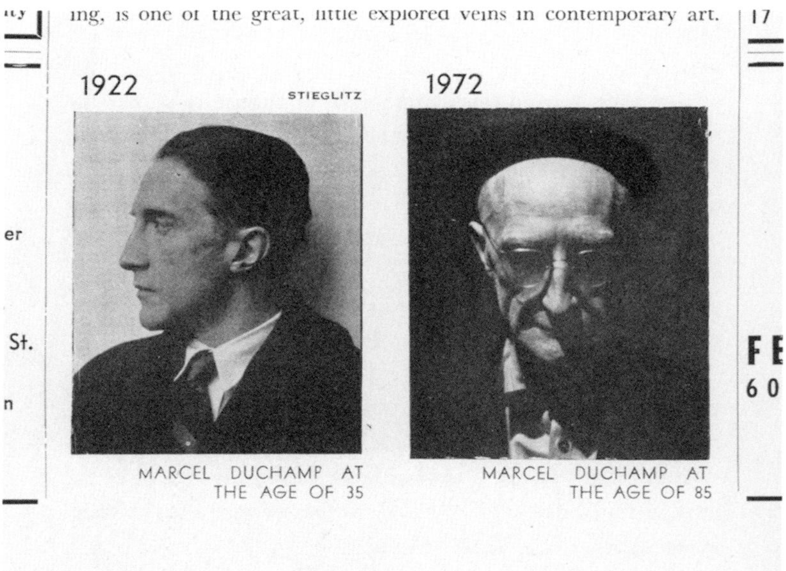

View. Marcel Duchamp Number, March 1945.
Last page (detail)

Marcel Duchamp at the Age of 85

An Incunabulum of Conceptual Photography

Works that are not art

In 1945, in an essay published in the American avant-garde magazine *View*, Harriet and Sidney Janis observed that while Marcel Duchamp had "stopped painting more than twenty years ago" new works "continue[d] to come into being," but these works were "so unorthodox and so far removed from (...) painting and sculpture" that they were "scarcely recognizable as the products of creative activity."[1] It was indeed the case that Duchamp had during the previous two decades been exercising his artistic fantasy on tasks that at that time did not count as art, such as the fabrication of optical toys (*Rotoreliefs*), the installation of a doorway for a gallery (*Porte de Gradiva*), the making of a pocket chess set, the designing of book and magazine covers, the organizing and designing of exhibitions, the dressing of shop windows, and the invention of a portable museum in a suitcase (*Boîte-en-valise*).[2] Duchamp's activity in these artistically ephemeral fields of creativity were guided by a thought that he had already noted down, in the form of a question, as early as 1913: "Can one make works that are not art?"[3] One of Duchamp's most remarkable works, which for almost half a century was not in fact recognized as a work of art, was published in the "Marcel Duchamp Number" of the magazine *View*, and in the very same issue as the one in which the Janises had published their clairvoyant observations.

The work in question was a photographed self-portrait of Duchamp, which was featured at the end of the magazine as the culmination of a dozen articles on his work penned by befriended artists, writers, critics, and dealers. Of modest format, barely larger than a passport photo (5.5 × 4.6 cm), the photograph shows the introverted, somewhat melancholic physiognomy of an old man.[4] The face is illuminated not from the front or the side, as is usual in portrait photography, but from above and at a steep angle. A beret, which covers the subject's hair and seems to hover over his high forehead like a black halo, lends the face a mask-like appearance. Appropriately, in keeping with his apparently advanced age, Duchamp is wearing a pair of spectacles, the rims of which, by dint of the strong lighting, cast deep shadows on the lower part of his face and heighten the impression of gauntness. The dull lenses and the unshaven chin awaken associations with a somewhat unkempt old man. Duchamp is leaning his head slightly downwards, looking not in the direction of the camera but inwardly, as though he is already reconciled with the world. The caption of the portrait reads: "Marcel Duchamp at the Age of 85." At that time, however, Duchamp was only 58. How, then, was such a portrait possible? Duchamp's physiognomy seems completely natural. On account of the small format and the poor quality of print, there are no signs of make-up or disguise. Perhaps the indicated age of "85" is a misprint, a simple twist of numbers? The answer must be no, for this photograph does not stand alone in *View* but is paired with another portrait photograph taken by the famous photographer Alfred Stieglitz in 1922 and captioned "Marcel Duchamp at the Age of 35."[5] The years prominently indicated above the two photographs are 1922 and 1972 respectively. Thus our immediate confusion when confronted by these two photographs and their respective indications of age and year cannot but lead us to assume that the portrait of Duchamp in his dotage is a photograph from the future, from the year 1972, but this is not only technically infeasible but also biologically impossible, as Duchamp died in 1968.

That this portrait of Duchamp at the age of 85 meant more to Duchamp than the mere production of pictorial material for publication in *View* is underscored by the fact that he displayed the original photograph, mounted on white board, in the shop window of the New York bookshop Gotham Book Mart only a month after its publication in the said magazine.[6] The surrealist window display, which featured an almost naked female window dummy with a water tap protruding from her thigh, had been designed by Duchamp to mark the publication of André Breton's prose poem *Arcane 17*. It had first been installed in the shop window of the book publisher Brentano's, but angry protests from the League of Women necessitated its dismantling after only a few hours, whereupon it was reinstalled

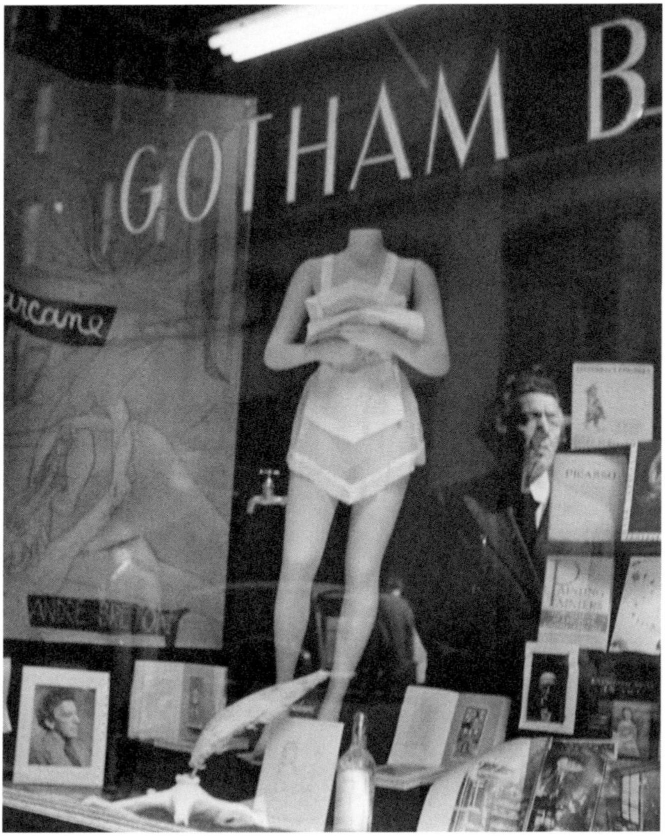

Marcel Duchamp, Window installation for *Arcane 17*, by André Breton, at *Gotham Book Mart*, 1945. Silver gelatin print, 19.6 × 15.7 cm. Centre Georges Pompidou, Bibliothèque Kandinsky. Displayed on the bottom right is the photograph *Marcel Duchamp at the Age of 85*.

in the shop window of the Gotham Book Mart in 47th Street, where it remained on show for an entire week.[7]

There is no knowledge of any documentary evidence to the effect that this portrait photograph was at the time regarded a work of art, nor is there any reference to any copyright or claim to authorship under the reproduction of the photograph in *View*. Thus it was that for many decades it remained unclear whether the photograph was a self-portrait or the work of a portrait photographer. It is mentioned neither in Robert Lebel's monograph *Sur Marcel Duchamp* of 1959, nor in Arturo Schwarz's catalogue raisonné *The Complete Works of Marcel Duchamp* of 1968, nor was it exhibited in the large retrospectives at the Museum of Modern Art and the Philadelphia Museum of Art in 1973 and the Musée National d'art moderne at the Centre Pompidou in 1977. The exhibition catalogue of the Museum of Modern Art and the Philadelphia Museum of Art clearly reveal the status that this portrait photograph "enjoyed" at that time. As the curators of the exhibition obviously did not know what to make of this extraordinary photograph from the future and, moreover, refused to recognize it as a self-portrait of Duchamp, it was not included in the exhibition but simply placed among the illustrations in the "Chronology" section.[8] There was, however, one exception in the long history of disregard for this witty and ephemeral work of art: in the spring of 1958, the Paris surrealist painter and essayist, Marcel Jean, had embarked upon a research trip across the United States in preparation for a book on Surrealism and stayed a whole week in New York with Marcel and Alexina Duchamp in their apartment at 327 East 28th Street.[9] Together they visited Philadelphia in order to view the large Arensberg Collection of Duchamp's works at the Philadelphia Museum of Art and also the Barnes Collection in nearby Merion. As a parting gift, Duchamp gave him an original print of his portrait "at the age of 85" and a reproduction of his portrait taken by Stieglitz in 1923.[10] While the fact that he made a gift of both photographs clearly shows how important their dual publication in *View* actually was for Duchamp, this concept was not observed by Marcel Jean when he published his book *Histoire de la peinture surréaliste*, for the portrait "at the age of 85" was published without the Stieglitz portrait.[11] What is quite remarkable, however, is that this portrait was not integrated into the copy, as was usually the case with the portraits of most of the other artists, but rather placed on a double page together with paintings by Picabia, Man Ray, Magritte among others.

The portrait in Marcel Jean's possession is a variant of the portrait illustrated in *View*. The pose, facial expression, lighting, and taking angle are the same on both photographs, but Duchamp is not wearing spectacles on this photograph, contrary to the photograph published in *View*.[12] This tiny detail makes an enormous difference. While in the portrait in *View* the face is partially hidden by the spectacles and the shadows cast by them blur the subject's physiognomy, the facial features on the photograph without the spectacles are clear and even. The beret creates the impression that the subject's high, ghastly pale forehead does not extend beyond the hairline, such that the face is so shaped that it seems to end at the outer contour of the brow, awakening associations with a life or death mask. Such associations are strengthened by the fact that the subject's gaze is not directed towards the lens of the camera, that is to say, towards an imaginary viewer, but rather inwardly, with his head bowed slightly in the manner of an aged, ascetic thinker. His eye sockets are so much in shadow that it is difficult to make out whether the eyes are open or even completely closed. Unlike the portrait in *View*, this portrait makes Duchamp's face appear

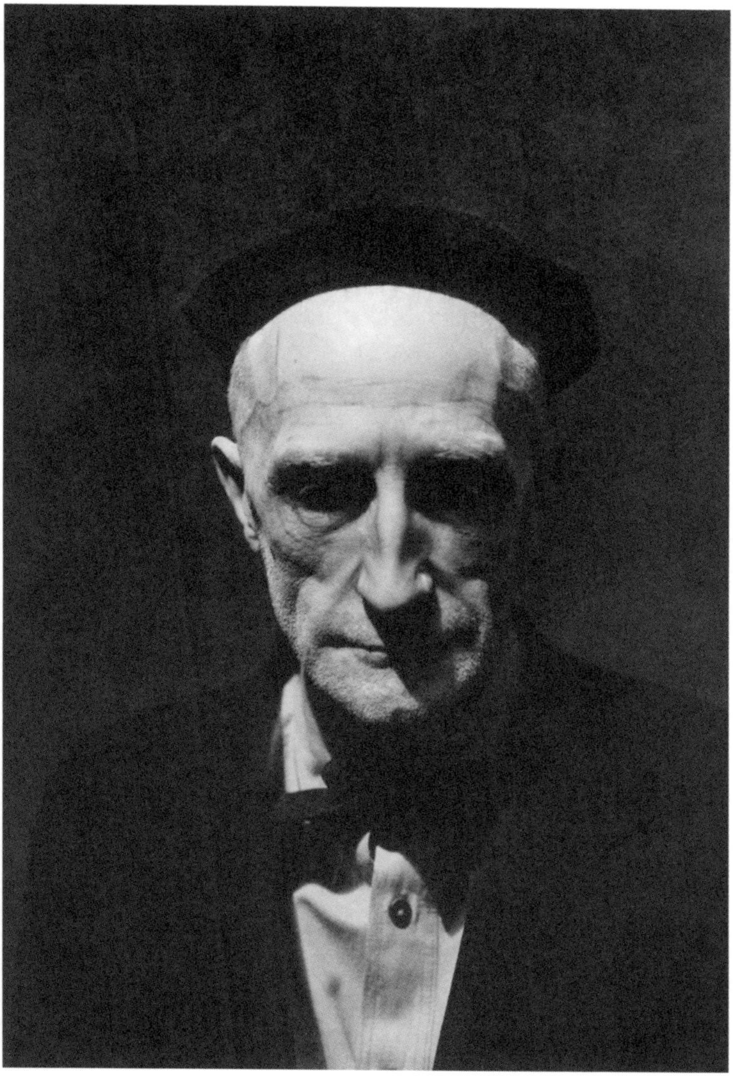

Marcel Duchamp at the Age of 85, 1945. Photo: Percy Rainford.
Silver gelatin print, 16.8 × 11.9 cm. Private Collection.

spiritualized to a high degree, though this is ascribable less to the subject's concentrated, inwardly directed mien than to the peculiarity of the lighting, which created the impression that his face was shining from within.

After the original print from Marcel Jean's collection had been exhibited in the *Marcel Duchamp* exhibition at the Ronny Van de Velde Gallery in Antwerp in 1991,[13] Arturo Schwarz included the same portrait photograph in his revised and extended catalogue raisonné on Marcel Duchamp in 1996, but not without committing two factual errors.[14] Firstly, it was not this photograph that had been reproduced in *View* but a variant with spectacles and, secondly, the photograph was not an "anonymous photograph" thought to have been appropriated by Duchamp because it bore certain physiognomic similarities to him.[15] After the author's discussion of "Marcel Duchamp at the Age of 85" in his essay "Die Fotografie des Möglichen. Von Marcel Duchamp bis Anna und Bernhard Blume" [Photography of the Possible. From Marcel Duchamp to Anna and Bernhard Blume] in 1999 against the foil of Duchamp's technique of the staged self-portrait and his so-called "compensation portraits," and, three years later, its full-page reproduction in the catalogue of the exhibition *Marcel Duchamp* at the Jean Tinguely Museum in Basel,[16] the portrait photograph has been exhibited and reproduced on many occasions[17] and also been frequently discussed in the literature on Duchamp.[18] The original print of the portrait published in *View*, measuring 17 × 11.6 cm and showing Duchamp wearing spectacles, had remained in Duchamp's possession until his death and was shown for the first time in the exhibition *Inventing Marcel Duchamp: The Dynamics of Portraiture* at the National Portrait Gallery in Washington in 2009.[19] Following the death of Duchamp's widow in 1995, the print was donated by her children, Jacqueline, Paul, and Peter Matisse, in memory of their mother, to the Philadelphia Museum of Art. A comparison with the original print showed that the head-and-shoulder portrait published in *View* had been cropped on all four sides.

Right up until the present, the portrait has puzzled Duchamp scholars. Who was the photographer? Did he take it himself with the aid of a self-timer? How did he manage to make himself look twenty-seven years older so convincingly?

Without any relevant sources, these questions could be answered only on the basis of speculation. Arturo Schwarz, the author of the catalogue raisonné on Duchamp, ventured the theory that the subject of the portrait was not Marcel Duchamp at all but rather a complete stranger who just looked like him. The artist, he writes, had simply found the portrait photograph in 1945 and published it in *View* as a self-portrait "at the age of 85." Duchamp's biographer Bernard Marcadé can explain Duchamp's suddenly aged appearance only on the assumption that the photograph was heavily retouched.[20] There are, however, no signs of any retouching on either of the original prints. Judith Housez assumes in her Duchamp biography of 2006 that the photograph is a montage,[21] but neither of the original prints manifests the typically sharp edges of a negative or positive photomontage or any typical signs of multiple exposure.

It was Michael Taylor, the former curator of modern art at the Philadephia Museum of Art, who in 2009 identified the New York photographer Percy Rainford as the photographer who took the photographs.[22] After studying the original print in the museum's collection and noticing the white, powdery particles on the chin stubble, eyebrows, and hairline, Taylor put forward the theory that the portrait photograph must have something to do with the making of Duchamp's life mask, which the New York sculptor and life-casting specialist, Ettore

Salvatore, had made at some hitherto unknown point in time. He assumed that the portrait "at the age of 85" had been taken immediately after removal of the mask, "as Duchamp's face, stubble, and hairline reveal traces of a powdery substance consistent with the plaster that would have been used for his life mask"[23] and consequently dates the making of the life mask to the same year as that of the photograph.[24] While Taylor had correctly identified the photographer of the portraits of "Marcel Duchamp at the Age of 85," his speculations as to how and why the photographs were taken took a wrong turn, as Frederick Kiesler's never-before-published draft article in the appendix to this publication proves. Kiesler had assisted Duchamp with his self-portrayal in Percy Rainford's studio. In a ten-page typescript, which is kept in the archive of the Austrian Frederick and Lillian Kiesler Private Foundation in Vienna, Kiesler gives a detailed acount of how Duchamp uses a black eyeliner pencil and white powder to lend his face the features of an old man and, accoutred with black tie and beret, struck the pose of an old, ascetic artist, deeply sunk in thought.

Frederick Kiesler's draft article "I was waiting for Marcel ..."

Around the time the photograph was taken, Duchamp was a close friend of the architect, artist, and designer Frederick Kiesler. They had probably first gotten to know one another in 1925,[25] but their acquaintanceship did not turn into friendship until 1937, when Kiesler published such a precise and well-founded analysis of the *Large Glass*[26] that Duchamp saw in him a like-minded thinker and artist.[27] When Duchamp emigrated from occupied France to New York in June 1942, he first stayed as a lodger, until October 1943, with Stefi and Frederick Kiesler in their penthouse on Seventh Avenue. This was the beginning of an intensive exchange and close collaboration between the two artists, which was to last a whole six years.[28] For the opening exhibition of Peggy Guggenheim's Gallery, *Art of this Century*, in autumn 1942, for example, Kiesler invented a new kind of viewing device for Duchamp's most recent work, the *Boîte-en-valise* [The Box in a Valise].[29] In the following year they together published the so-called "Twin Touch Test" in *VVV* magazine (nos. 2–3). With this test, the reader was supposed to let the fingertips of both hands glide to and fro over a piece of chicken wire, which was shaped like a female torso and inserted into the back of the cover, and to continue doing so until he could answer the question: "Is it an unusual feeling of touch?"[30] Five prizes were to go to the best readers' descriptions of the feeling of touch experienced during the test. Kiesler's contribution to this experiment was probably limited to the wording of the prize offer that accompanied the test, while the actual test object on the back cover of the magazine had doubtless been conceived by Duchamp,[31] for it was precisely of the same ilk as the artistic experiments he was carrying out at that time on sensations experienced at the very limits of human perception, for which he had coined the term "infra-mince" [infra-thin].[32] The "Twin Touch Test" typically exploits the phenomenon by which, after gliding to and fro over a piece of chicken wire, the fingertips of one hand and those of the other feel like the surfaces of foreign bodies when they subsequently touch one another. In matters concerning such experiments of perception, Kiesler was probably Duchamp's most competent artistic interlocutor in New York at that time, as he had been the initiator and director of the *Laboratory for Design Correlation* at Columbia University between the years of 1937 and 1942 and as such was intensively involved in the psychology of visual perception.[33]

When the publishers of *View* magazine informed him in December 1944 that they were planning a Duchamp Number for March of the following year, Duchamp immediately involved Kiesler in this project. On the 22nd of the same month they met in the editor's office in order to discuss the concept of the planned *View* issue.[34] Duchamp then asked a good dozen befriended artists, writers, dealers, and curators to contribute to it.[35] Judging from a letter written by Duchamp to Henri-Pierre Roché, the preparations for this issue during the first months of 1945 were evidently Duchamp's most important artistic activity. "I have succeeded in living here almost like in Paris, i.e., in avoiding public life (exhibitions, cocktails, parties)," he writes to his friend in Paris. "Nonetheless, I have had to help with the production of an issue of 'View'."[36] On the six pages allocated to him by the editors of the magazine, Kiesler produced a kind of "correalistic" portrait of Marcel Duchamp entitled *Poème espace dédié à H(ieronymous) Duchamp* [Space poem dedicated to H(ieronymous) Duchamp].[37] It was a complicated photomontage in the form of a triptych featuring a number of fold-out pages and showing Duchamp in his new studio in 14th Street, living and working like a hermit in the chaos of a cell overflowing with tools, garbage, and daily clutter. No other portrait in *View* came anywhere near this photomontage in terms of intellectual complexity and painstaking printing skill. Extending the Surrealist technique of the object poem [*poème objet*] into the three-dimensional, Kiesler created from a large number of photographs of the city of New York, of Duchamp's studio, and his window works the fascinating image of a poetical space in which everything merged together: indoors and outdoors, the studio and the city, the human being and his surroundings. Flanked by his window works *Fresh Widow* and *Brawl at Austerlitz* on the outside walls, Duchamp, the calming influence in this complex weave of real and imaginary lines of force, seems to be living in the middle of the *Large Glass*.[38] The photomontage is integrated into an intellectual portrait in the style of visual poetry that represents, with the aid of hieroglyphics, chess diagrams, and "line pictures," Duchamp on three further pages as an "artiste-inventeur" inspired by the logic of chess who has his equal in no one but Raymond Roussel.[39] As the typescript informs us, Kiesler had the necessary studio photographs for this photomontage taken by Percy Rainford on January 11, 1945, the very same photographer to whose studio he then came two days later in order to collect the prints[40] and also to assist Duchamp with the taking of his self-portrait "at the age of 85."

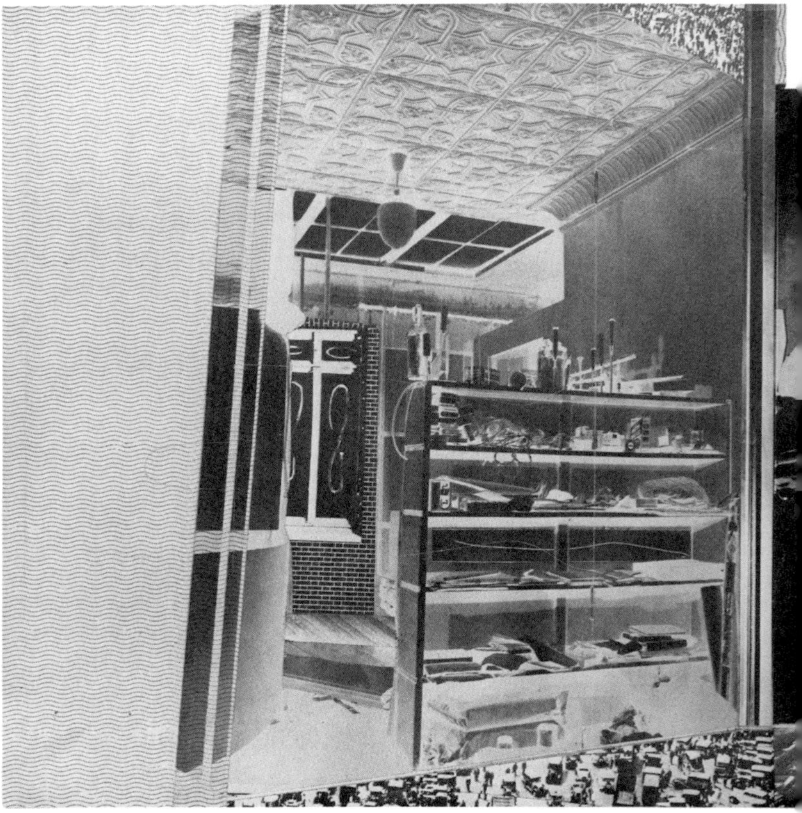

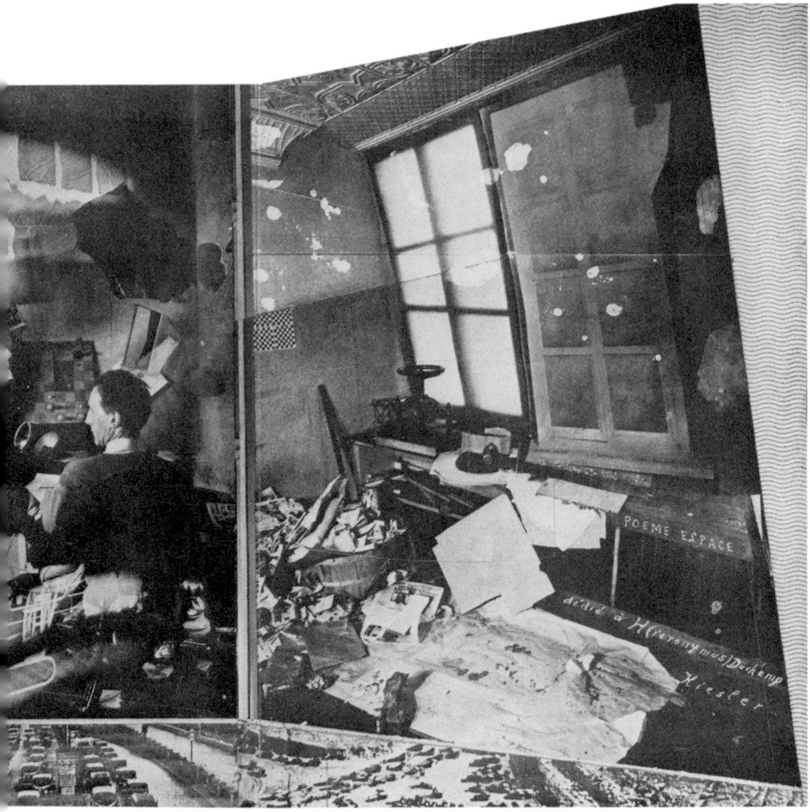

Frederick Kiesler: *Poème espace dédié à H(ieronymus) Duchamp*, photomontage in *View*, 1945. Recognizable on the shelf, top left, is the Bordeaux bottle prepared by Duchamp for the *View* cover.

According to an advertisement in a 1937 issue of *Art Digest*, Percy Rainford was a freelance photographer "specializing in works of art, interiors."[41] Numerous American museum archives contain photographs of works of art taken by Rainford. Duchamp, too, had occasionally availed himself of his services for the reproduction of art works, as evidenced by several prints in the "Alexina and Marcel Duchamp Papers" at the Philadelphia Museum of Art.[42] Rainford, who was appreciated as a particularly low-cost reproduction photographer, had between the years of 1942 and 1944 supplied photographic copywork for *VVV* magazine, whose "editorial advisers" also included Duchamp.[43] Duchamp met Rainford and Kiesler on January 1, for a two-hour discussion, probably about, among other things, the preparations for the photo session in his studio on January 11.[44] Thus Duchamp was already well acquainted with Rainford when he came to the photographer's studio on January 13, 1945 for the taking of the fictitiously aged portrait.

Kiesler remembers Rainford as a white-skinned Afro-American, "a Negro with a certain paleness, the down of a white man's skin. A combination which pleases both races."[45] This may explain why Rainford had since the 1920s been able to practise his profession in the American art scene without any problems. According to Kiesler's typescript, Rainford had two men in his employment in 1945, a young Afro-American apprentice and a laboratory assistant.[46] Rainford lived and worked in a studio located in an old brownstone on 57th Street, "with no name-card in the entrance hall, semi-anonymously, perched at the very end of a sinister corridor, in one room and two niches, one used for developing and one for printing, the whole habitat half artist's studio, half machine shop, lit by one meager window looking out into the prison yard formed by crumbling apartment houses leaning on one another."[47] At the very beginning of his typescript, Kiesler describes the antiquated, gas-fired drying machine on which the wet prints were dried.[48] Evidently just as old as this "toasting machine"[49] was the antediluvian large-format studio camera, "the type you see only in posters advertising portrait photography on boardwalks or in Luna Parks," the type of camera on which the cassette had to be changed after each photograph.[50] Anyone reading Kiesler's account cannot but be surprised at the haste in which Duchamp left the studio, with the two finished prints, immediately after the portrait sitting. The entire operation cannot have lasted even an hour. Duchamp had arrived at 5.35 p.m. and left the studio again around 6.15 p.m., as he had to be "downtown" at 7.00 p.m., but first had to go back to his apartment in 14th Street in order to remove his make-up, shave off his stubble, and change into other clothes.[51] The prints were probably contact prints from sheet film, which could be easily developed and dried in twenty to thirty minutes.[52] That Rainford did in fact make only one contact print from each of the negatives, which also tallies with the surviving originals,[53] is substantiated by a sentence in Kiesler's typescript: "(…) out came the photographer, laughing, the palms of his two hands holding towards us two dripping prints of the photographs he had taken a few minutes before."[54]

In his diary of 1959, Kiesler gives a revealing characterization of Percy Rainford's style as a portrait photographer: "He is the only photographer I know who portrays with sharpness and exactitude what the camera, not his own eye, sees, and that is a very rare quality in times such as ours when every member of our society not only believes in himself as a great personality, but also forces any type of mechanical equipment to show personality too."[55] This objectivity of style was probably one of the reasons – the other reason doubtless being the photographer's reasonable fees – why Duchamp decided to have his portrait "at the age of 85" taken by Rainford. He had no need for any subjective interpretation of his person by the photographer – this he could furnish himself with the aid of make-up and disguise – but simply a technically precise photograph. It is not least for this reason that Rainford is in Duchamp's eyes not the author of the photograph but merely the operator of the camera. Indeed, Kiesler's account of the portrait sitting in Rainford's studio clearly states that Duchamp had taken all the creative decisions himself. He was in complete charge, both over the transformation of his face with the aid of the make-up and the beret and over the choice of lighting and background. Kiesler writes: "He [the photographer] was now putting up a roll of white paper in the background; Marcel interrupted him – and me in my make-up work – and asked for a black background.[56] (...) Marcel insisted that the light must come from high up so as to make the shadows in the face sharp."[57] Having read Kiesler's account, we can now understand why Duchamp did not declare Percy Rainford as the author of the portrait "Marcel Duchamp at the Age of 85" in *View* magazine, while the other portrait taken in 1923 was clearly acknowledged as Stieglitz's work. Duchamp clearly considered this portrait to be a self-portrait, the photographer assisting only in a technical and not in an artistic sense.

Kiesler's typescript is not merely a memorandum for some later reference but the draft of a planned article, as the typescript itself clearly states in the passage describing Duchamp's preparations for the *View* cover: "You [Duchamp] said you would then have a print made from the tiny block, enlarge it to this magazine's format of 7 by 10 (...)" – a sentence from which it is clear that the article was to be published in "this magazine," that is to say, in the Duchamp number.[58] At the end of the typescript, the author asks Duchamp: "As they are unfortunately illegible on the bottle, may I now ask your permission to reproduce *in this article* [my italics] the personal particulars of your military document (...)? 'But of course,' Marcel replied. And here is the document."[59] Thus the article was to end with a legible reproduction of the page of Duchamp's military ID pass containing his personal particulars (see illustration on page 106), which had been printed on the label of the bottle featured on the front cover but then rendered illegible through the use of a coarse half-tone screen.

Duchamp's discussion with Kiesler about the possibility of using the personal particulars of his military ID pass from the period before the First World War as an illustration of a biographical article on the artist is echoed in the writings found after Duchamp's death. In a note that probably dates from the time when he was working on the special issue of *View*, Duchamp writes: "Episodic catalogue. Title page – reproduction 1st page of military ID pass – / arranged according to years – changes of location and pictures done in the year / for those not reproduced in the box perhaps indicate not reproduced / Only for the limited edition 10 or 15 copies."[60] While Kiesler had planned to use the first page of Duchamp's military ID pass as the final illustration for his article in *View*, Duchamp is apparently reflecting here on the possibility of using it for the title page of a catalogue of his works, a catalogue that would accompany the limited edition of the magazine and feature in particular a chronological arrangement of the artist's works according to his episodic travels and changes of abode.[61] When he was asked by his friend Henri-Pierre Roché eight years later to submit a suggestion for the cover of the book *Souvenirs sur Marcel Duchamp* on which he, Roché, was working at the time, Duchamp fell back on his idea of 1945 and sent Roché a photo-

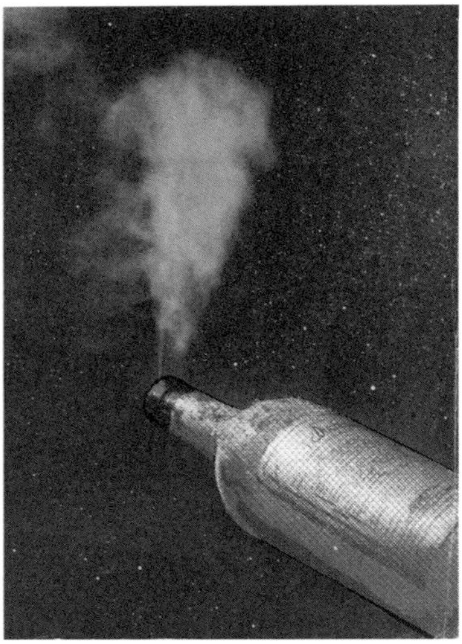

View,
Marcel Duchamp
Number, March 1945.
Front cover
(detail)

graph of the first page of his military ID pass, recommending that he depict it on the front cover exactly as it was, "including the much-thumbed corners."[62] This planned publication, however, never reached fruition.

As regards its content, Kiesler's typescript comprises two parts. The first two thirds concern the staging and taking of the portrait of "Marcel Duchamp at the Age of 85" and the last third describes the preparation of a Bordeaux bottle in Duchamp's studio, its photographic reproduction by Percy Rainford and the complicated halftone screening of this reproduction for the photomontage on the front cover of *View*. As regards its style, the article reads like a "making-of" of Duchamp's pictorial contributions to the special number of *View*. Using reportage-like language, the author takes the reader "behind the scenes" and describes from the perspective of a friend and close confidant of the artist how the imaginary self-portrait of Duchamp in his dotage and the enigmatic cover image of a smoking wine bottle against a nocturnal, starry sky were actually made. Kiesler's chosen place for the narrative is the studio of the photographer Percy Rainford, where the time lines of the preceding three weeks of his and Duchamp's work for the Duchamp number of *View* now converge. Rainford is nowhere mentioned by name, only as "the photographer."[63] Kiesler and Duchamp meet in his studio in order to collect the prints of the photographs Rainford took for them a few days previously. Duchamp also wishes to have contact prints made from a roll of film and, much more importantly, to have his portrait taken "at the age of 85."

Just as Kiesler visually combines in the aforementioned "space poem" real and fictitious, indoor and outdoor spaces into an imaginary environment, so too does he link in the draft of his article different levels of time and weaves into the description of the making-up and photographing of Duchamp in his dotage an account of both past and planned activities, enabling the reader to learn something about Duchamp's other projects for this special number of *View*: about the enigmatic image for the magazine cover and also about the planned – though not realized – idea of printing consecutively on each page of the magazine a contact print of one of the seventy-two negatives of a roll of film, which would then give the effect of a moving picture – after the fashion of a flicker book – when the reader rapidly flipped through the pages of the magazine. What was actually shown on the film is not known.[64] Kiesler's draft article affords the reader an insight into the making of Duchamp's pictorial contributions to the magazine at a moment when things were still in a state of flux and nothing had been decided in detail.

What cannot fail to astonish us about Duchamp's way of working is the simplicity of the means with which he is able to create the most enigmatic of images: a bottle, some glue, some powdered cardboard, and a page from a military ID pass for the magazine cover; some white powder, an eyeliner pencil, and a three-day beard for an imaginary old-age portrait.

The draft article was probably written relatively soon after the portrait sitting. Duchamp had still spoken during the sitting about having himself photographed at the age of 84. Had Kiesler already been informed about Duchamp's intention to change his age to 85, he would certainly have mentioned it. The fact that he did not even correct this detail later is in itself an indication that the article was intended for the Marcel Duchamp Number of *View* and, after its publication, had lost its relevance. The fact that Duchamp, at the end of the script, grants Kiesler permission to print the page of his military ID pass, on which the label of the Bordeaux bottle had been based, supports the theory that he had been initiated into the article project from the very beginning. What actually happened between the drafting of the script and the printing of the Marcel Duchamp Number, and why the article was not published in the end, cannot be reconstructed from existing source material. That the editors were in fact interested in an article in the style of a "making-of" of Duchamp's pictorial contributions to an issue specially devoted to his life and work is proven by a small column on the inner title page entitled "I Cover the Cover," in which Peter Lindamood, a journalistically active army corporal and a friend of the editor Charles Henri Ford, imparts to the reader details of the making of the cover montage as described by Kiesler in his article draft, adding a few more details and making them out to be personal information from Marcel Duchamp himself.[65] Asked fifty-five years later, Ford could not remember the circumstances surrounding the planning and publication of the Duchamp number.[66] The only thing that was indelibly imprinted on his memory was the enormous cost of printing the triptych photomontage: "It cost a lot of money. I think it broke our budget."[67] The size and scope of *View* differed considerably from one issue to the next, depending on the available funds and contributions. The issue that had preceded the Duchamp number was forty-eight pages thick,[68] while the one that followed it contained only thirty pages.[69] Although the 54-page Duchamp number was one of the largest issues of *View*, there was apparently no longer any space for Kiesler's lengthy article following the influx of all the essays by Duchamp's friends and admirers, but only for a narrow column like that of Peter Lindamood's on the inner title page. After all, Kiesler was, both as an author and an artist, already more present than any other contributor, for his "correalistic" Duchamp portrait covered a whole six pages. Instead of his long article, Kiesler then published a brief commentary on his photomontage entitled "Les Larves d'Imagie d'Henri Robert Marcel Duchamp" [Henri Robert Marcel Duchamp's World of Images in its Larva State].[70] Here Kiesler utilized Duchamp's other forenames, Henri and Robert, the existence of which – according to his typescript – had been unknown to him until he read the personal particulars of Duchamp's military ID pass used for the label of the Bordeaux bottle.[71]

Kiesler begins his draft article with the suspenseful sentence: "I was waiting for Marcel – it was 5.35 p.m. at 42 West 57 Str., January 13, 1945."[72] Evidently Kiesler had arranged to meet Duchamp in Rainford's studio. But why? Had he been let in on Duchamp's plans? That this might not have been the case is suggested by Kiesler's surprise at Duchamp's pale, sickly appearance: "At that very moment I heard the door open and Marcel was in the room. His hair was grey. He looked ill. 'Marcel, are you all right?' 'I have to look even worse. I must look like 84,' he answered. He had [taken] out of his pocket 1 powder compact, 1 eyeliner pencil, 1 clean and neatly folded handkerchief, 1 pair of gold-rimmed spectacles and a beret. Now I understood. He had come to have his portrait taken at the age of 84."[73] On the other hand, the rapidity with which he "understood" and the fact that, in the ensuing dialogue, Duchamp involved Kiesler in his portrait project entirely as a matter of course suggest quite clearly that Kiesler was familiar with Duchamp's plans.

Duchamp had arranged to meet Kiesler in Rainford's studio because he needed him to help him with his make-up. "'You'll have to help me finish my make-up.' I accompanied Marcel into the other room, which looked like a cave, unfurnished except for a roller blind that hung down askew, an iron bedstead with a blue blanket and a large mirror on the wall, illuminated by a naked electric light, in front of which Marcel was already standing. We studied his face in the mirror for a few seconds and then another few seconds later we were back in the room. Marcel sat broadly in the chair, his head leant back, as though he were at the barber's. I grabbed the white handkerchief, wiped those parts of his hair and face that were too white and dusted the white powder off his black tie. (...) A few black lines across his brow, a deepening of the nasolabial folds, which Marcel had already deepened slightly, a powdering of the ears, which we had forgotten, thin black lines on both edges of the nose and at the end of the nasal cartilage."[74] Indeed, the make-up had been applied so cleverly and skilfully that it is recognizable as such only with the aid of a magnifying glass. The rapidity with which Duchamp's facial expression was checked in the mirror and then finished with make-up tells us how carefully Duchamp had prepared the action before leaving his studio.

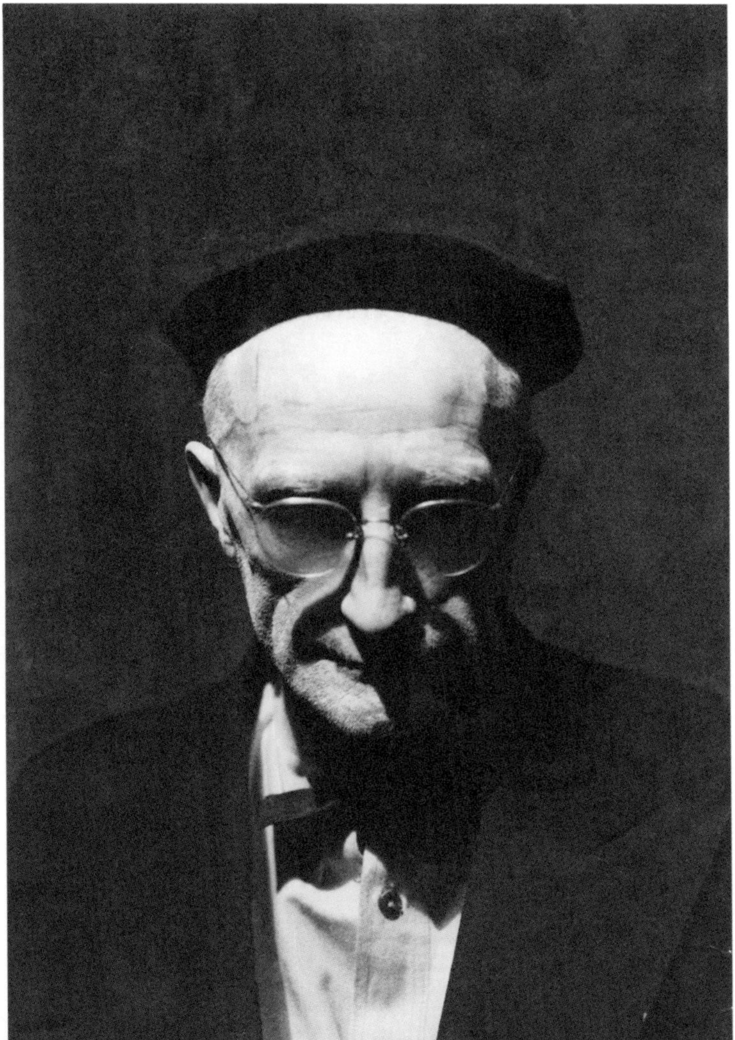

Marcel Duchamp at the Age of 85, 1945. Photo: Percy Rainford. Silver gelatin print, 17 × 11.6 cm. Philadelphia Museum of Art, Pennsylvania, Marcel Duchamp Archive: gift of Jacqueline, Paul, and Peter Matisse in memory of their mother, Alexina Duchamp.

This preparation consisted particularly in shaving the entire width of the brow along the hairline and the temples. Percy Rainford's studio had for the time being been turned into a theatrical stage or a film set, where Kiesler had assumed the responsibilities of a make-up artist and set designer. Once work on the make-up was finished, the "actor's" pose and facial expression had to be checked before the camera. "Marcel struck his grinning pose once more, but asked me to keep a close watch on the sunken lines around the mouth, as he would now widen and narrow them. I was to decide what was not too wide and not too narrow for an old man of 84."[75] It would seem that Duchamp did not hit upon the idea of changing his age from 84 to 85 until the final layout stage of the project when his fictitiously aged portrait was placed next the portrait taken by Stieglitz. As Duchamp's birthday was July 28 and he had decided on a significant time gap of half a century between the two portraits (1922–1972), his age on January 13, 1972 would indeed have been only 84. However, when formulating the captions for the two portraits, Duchamp completely waived documentary accuracy, for the age of 85 was far more ambiguous. As Duchamp's friends, and certainly most *View* readers, would have known that he had not yet reached the end of his life in 1945, they could easily have taken the obvious mistake in age to be a simple twist of numbers, a typesetting error. Duchamp had at that time reached the age of 58 and not 85.

Two portraits were taken, one with spectacles and one without.[76] The pose, the facial expression, and the framing of the image – i. e., the distance from the camera to the subject – were the same. Kiesler's observation that "the lenses of the spectacles were smeared and powdered (Marcel had evidently already prepared them in his studio)"[77] clearly shows how painstaking Duchamp's preparations for his self-portrayal as an old man had actually been. The smeared lenses are clearly discernible on the original print in the collection of the Philadelphia Museum of Art. The dull, virtually opaque lenses not only hamper our view of the subject's eyes but also suggest that the old man possibly lives alone and can no longer look after his spectacles properly. Before the photograph was taken, Duchamp was unsure "whether 84 would come out better with or without glasses." As soon as Duchamp is given the contact prints, he asks his "make-up artist" Kiesler: "Which one shall we use?"[78] His use of the word "use" is only a minor linguistic detail, but one that doubtless refers to its publication in *View* and, by the same token, shows how well Kiesler had been familiarized with the project. All the same, Duchamp's question is more rhetorical than curious, for he continues without pausing: "The one with glasses looks like 84, the one without only like 79."[79] While opinions may of course differ when it comes to interpreting the features of old age, one cannot but agree that the portrait *with* spectacles looks less contrived than the portrait *without* spectacles, for it does in fact look like an ordinary portrait photograph of an ordinary old man, while the spiritualized physiognomy of the subject without spectacles awakens associations with an ancient ascetic philosopher, its mask-like appearance strangely seeming to transport him into a world beyond real time. The beret covering Duchamp's hair and the unusual – for a portrait – frontal illumination of his brow transforms Duchamp's head into a flat face mask reminiscent, not least through the sunken cheeks and tightly pressed lips, of photographs of death masks.[80] Perhaps it was precisely the close association with the aesthetic of the death mask that went too far for Duchamp, at least for the publication in *View*, and induced him to choose the "more commonplace" bespectacled portrait. After all, Duchamp wanted to pair the portrait taken by Stieglitz in 1922 not with the mask

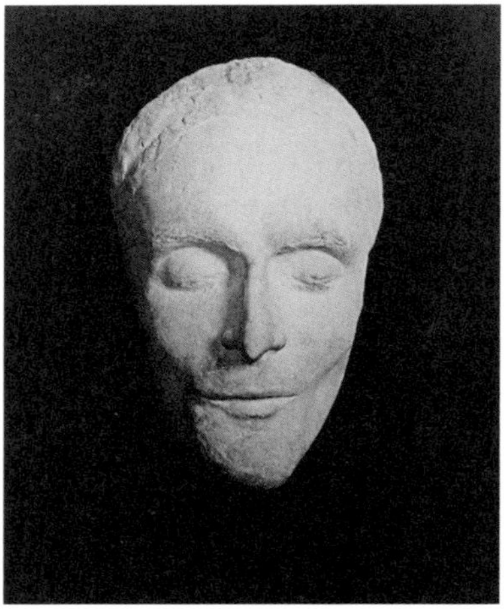

Death mask
of Modigliani, 1929.
Photo: Man Ray

of a dead man but rather with the portrait of a man who had aged a good fifty years. The reduction of the print to the size of passport photo and the lack of detail in its deep black reproduction in the magazine suppressed all traces of make-up and further underscored the impression of an ordinary photograph – its only extraordinary feature being its portrayal of a person in the future.

"A little game between 'I' und 'me'."

When Duchamp was asked by the curator Katherine Kuh in 1961 why he had such a strong need to distance himself as far as possible from the traditional forms of expression, he replied: "I was really trying to invent, instead of merely expressing myself. I was never interested in looking at myself in an aesthetic mirror. My intention was always to get away from myself, though I knew perfectly well that I was using myself. Call it a little game between 'I' and 'me'."[81] In 1911, in the painting *Sad Young Man on a Train*, Duchamp had for the first time made his own person the theme of his art. 1917 saw a change in medium when he visited the Broadway Photo Shop in New York to have a five-way portrait taken.[82] Such "multiphotographs," which showed the subject simultaneously from the front, the back, and both sides and were produced with the aid of a relatively simple hinged-mirror trick, were part and parcel of the then popular genre of leisure and recreational photography.[83] Indeed, Roland Barthes recognized in the mirroring aspect of the photographic image one of its most important historical and aesthetic innovations. "Photography is the advent of myself as other, a cunning dissociation of the conscience of identity," he writes in *Camera lucida*.[84] For Duchamp, this splitting of his photographic identity into five different faces marked the beginning of a whole series of artistic self-projections in the

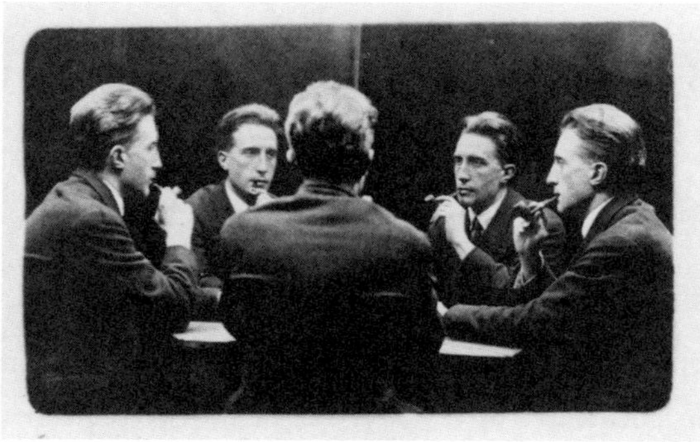

Marcel Duchamp, Multi-portrait, 1917. Photo: Broadway Photo Shop. 8.9 × 13.3 cm, Musée national d'art moderne, Centre Georges Pompidou.

medium of photography, culminating, and also terminating, in 1945 in his self-portrait at the age of 85. While Duchamp's masquerade portraits, mostly playful and mostly no bigger than a postcard, were indeed perceived as visual manifestations of the artist Marcel Duchamp, they were not considered as works of art. After all, their places of display were not art galleries or art museums but rather the pages of a periodical, a poster or the label of a perfume bottle.

One of the myths of modernism is the notion that the *Large Glass* and the readymades marked the beginning of the desubjectification of modern art. We may indeed consider this true as regards a work's inherent aesthetic, but not without reservation, for even if the artist disappeared entirely from his works, leaving no trace of his hand in their making, he could not escape public attention. On the contrary, there is hardly any other artist of the twentieth century who has been the object of profane veneration to the same extent as Marcel Duchamp. Once he had reached the front pages of the U.S. national dailies with his painting *Nude Descending a Staircase* in 1913 and, two years later, had emigrated to New York, the media began to take a very curious interest in the thoughts and ideas of an artist who not only seemed to be completely indifferent about success but had possibly discovered a new artistic language about which his fellow artists knew nothing. Duchamp reacted to the public's growing interest in his person by surprising it with regular changes of identity. In 1918 he painted his last oil painting (*Tu m'*); in 1923 he completed his work on the *Large Glass*; from 1920 until 1924 he devoted himself almost entirely to the design and fabrication of optical machines. So who was he? Evidently no longer a painter. So what was he *then*? Who was this unpredictable personality? The puzzles he set for his collectors, his friends, and a small, readily surveyable avant-garde scene were complemented by a series of photographic portraits that were just as enigmatic as his artistic actions and decisions.

Duchamp's greatest fame was reaped by his self-portrayals as *Rrose Sélavy*, photographed by his friend Man Ray in 1921. The name of his alter ego, with which Duchamp signed his works – often in conjunction with his real name – until 1942, is a pun that says it all: *Eros c'est la vie* – Eros, that's life. Duchamp was certainly familiar with Rimbaud's famous dictum "je est un autre" ["I is someone else"], but his photographic metamorphosis into a woman was not just an exploration of the "individual's inner world, of the psychical structure of identity"[85] but also, and equally so, a deliberate game of confusion with his persona. From 1921 Duchamp used the medium of the photographic self-portrait to bring into circulation ever new identities of himself, each one being yet a further side to the artistic individual who went by the name of Marcel Duchamp and/or *Rrose Sélavy*. That

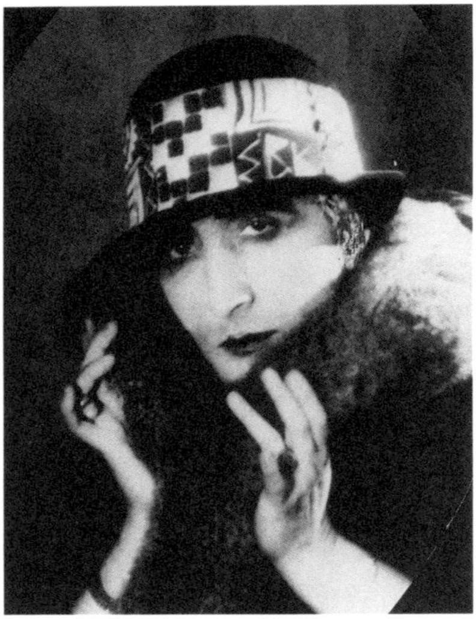

Rrose Sélavy, 1921.
Photo: Man Ray

the intention behind his photographic transformation into *Rrose Sélavy* was not to replace his male identity by a female one but rather to implement an aesthetic strategy aimed at a multiplication of identities is proved by the fact that in 1921 he not only disguised himself as a woman but also made an appearance as a "monk" amid members of the art public. The tonsure had been shaved into Duchamp's hair by the Mexican graphic artist and caricaturist, Georges de Zayas, then living in Paris.[86] Unlike the *Rrose Sélavy* portrait, this self-portrayal did not take place just in front of a camera. For several weeks – Dada was having its heyday in Paris at that time – Duchamp, thus tonsured, actually appeared in person within a small circle of friends.[87] A good half dozen photographs of this masquerade, taken by at least two different photographers, have survived.[88] The most representative among these photographs was again taken by Man Ray. Altogether contrary to Duchamp's "image" as a hardboiled, market-oriented strategist, which is how American art critics during the Pop Art era saw him, this self-portrayal discloses Duchamp's romantic ideal of the artist. Duchamp compared the life of an artist to that of a monk, "a lay monk, if you so wish, indeed, a very Rabelaisian one. But it is an ordination, no more and no less."[89] The tonsure, the symbol of the individual's subjugation to God, takes in Duchamp's case the form of a star-shaped comet, the tail of which is pointing forwards, a motif that harks back to a literary sketch of 1912 for a symbolist/futurist painting of a car journey (*Route Jura-Paris*). The protagonist of this sketch is a "headlight child", which "could, graphically, be a comet, which would have its tail in front."[90] And to make the game even more confusing, still in 1921, Duchamp cut out a small piece from his "tonsure" portrait and stuck it on Francis Picabia's painting *L'Œil cacodylate*, to which he then added the pun "en 6 qu'habilla rrose Sélavy," thus linking the

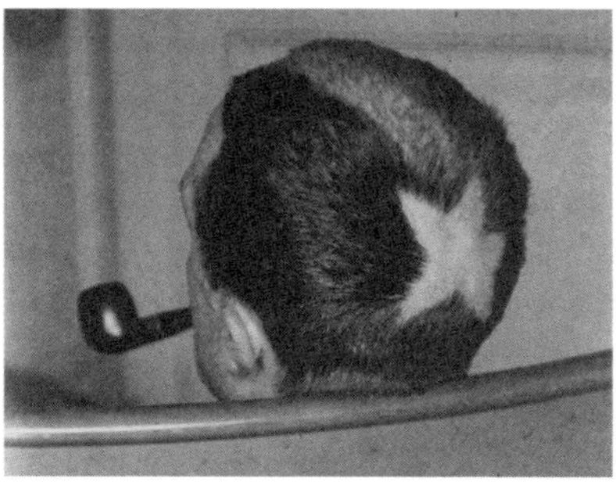

Tonsure, 1921.
Photo: Man Ray

"tonsure" portrait with the figure of Rrose Sélavy.[91] And so it was that Duchamp, in 1921, had assumed two new identities with the aid of such staged photographic self-portraits. First he transformed himself into a woman and then, only a short time later, back into a man, into an "artist-monk" with an enigmatic comet tonsure.[92]

Three years later, Duchamp again had his portrait taken by Man Ray, this time for a *Monte Carlo Bond* (*Obligation pour la roulette de Monte Carlo*).[93] This bond entitled the purchaser to a share in the winnings to be yielded by a roulette system at Monte Carlo. Using shaving cream in lieu of pomade, Duchamp shaped his hair for the portrait into wings reminiscent of the winged helmet of Hermes, the messenger of the Greek gods, who was famous for his shady dealings and was hence also the patron god of merchants – not excluding art dealers – and thieves. Duchamp sold each of these bonds for the tidy sum of 500 Francs and promised a dividend of 20%, but he was never able to pay it, as the system never yielded any winnings. The Monte Carlo Bond was much more profitable on the art market, where in the course of time its purchasing value increased a thousandfold.

While Duchamp loved self-presentations, disguises, and masquerades in front of the camera,[94] he strongly disliked being pigeonholed into a certain category of art by critics and fellow artists. The public recognition, the fame, that met him in the world of modern media, both verbally and visually, was seen by Duchamp as a constraining obligation to continue forever in the rut that success had brought with it. For decades, Duchamp was presented to the public not by name but as the man who, with his painting *Nude Descending a Staircase*, had provoked the biggest scandal in the more recent history of American art. When he said to Arturo Schwarz, "I don't want to be pinned

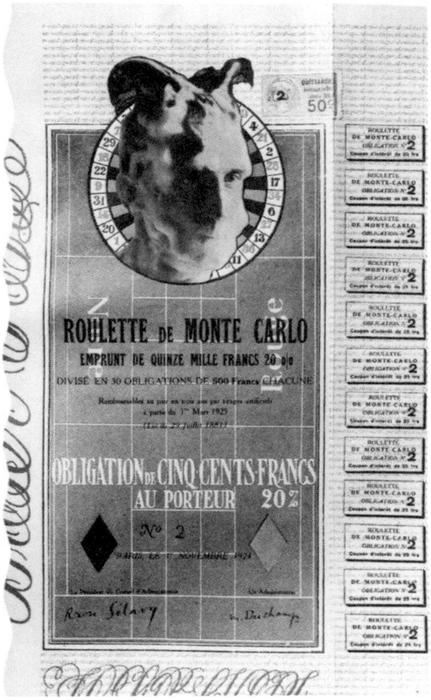

Monte Carlo Bond, 1924.
Photo: Man Ray

down to any position. My position is the lack of position," he was of course referring first and foremost to his work, but this remark held just as well for his understanding of himself as an artist.[95] Just as he constantly turned this way and that in his art so as not to be associated with any particular standpoint or movement, so too did he constantly change his public image by circulating his self-portrait in ever new disguises and aspects. As Duchamp saw things, the artist in the modern media-oriented society was constantly on the run from the madding crowd and from art agents of every description: critics, gallery owners, collectors, and art historians, all of them doing their utmost to nail him down as an exponent of a certain school or movement. This dialectic of self-portrayal and self-withdrawal, so typical of the modern artist's relationship to the public, was most aptly visualized by Duchamp in 1923 with his own artist's poster – *Wanted $2,000 Reward* – a joke wanted notice, found in a New York restaurant, on which he replaced the photographs of the originally wanted person by portraits of himself in typical mugshot fashion, one in profile, the other full face.[96] Behind the fictitious name of the fugitive, a certain George W. Welch, who had operated a "bucket shop" in New York under the name of HOOKE, LYON and CINQUER, Duchamp added the words: *Known also under the name RROSE SÉLAVY*. How deeply and indelibly the image of the hunter and the hunted was to imprint itself upon Duchamp's notion of the artist's relationship to the public is demonstrated by the fact that, forty years later, he placed the *WANTED* notice in the middle of the poster announcing his first retrospective exhibition at the Pasadena Art Museum.[97]

The two juxtaposed portraits in *View* – one taken in profile, the other full face – also echo, albeit distantly, Duchamp's wanted notice of 1923.[98] Indeed, it was the "Marcel Duchamp Number," the first monographic publication to be dedicated to his work, that did precisely what the artist himself abhorred: his person, his work, and his artistic standpoint were stamped, categorized, and shelved. In view of the large number of contributors – more than a dozen befriended artists, writers, critics, curators, and gallery owners had contributed essays to this issue – the reader ought to have expected a broad and richly facetted panorama of Duchamp's artistic endeavors and accomplishments. Instead, however, the descriptions of Duchamp's artistic identity in the various essays are astonishingly unani-

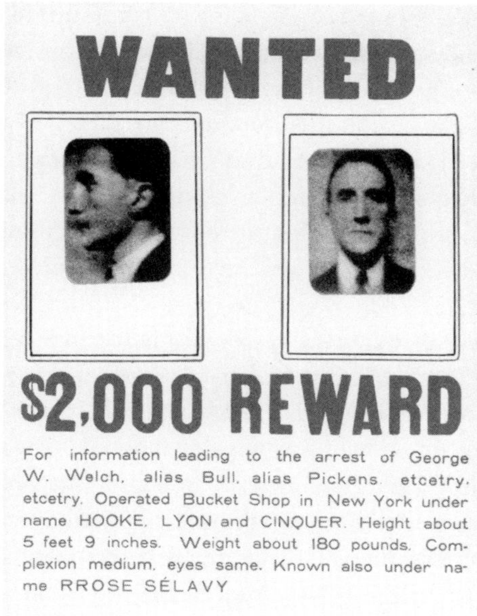

Wanted $2,000 Reward, 1923. Two-color offset lithograph, 20.7 × 16.2 cm, in: *The Box in a Valise*, 1941.

mous. The picture presented of Duchamp is that of a "has been," a painter who gave up painting twenty years ago and since then has been unable to find a new artistic agenda. With the exception of Breton's introduction, most of the articles are in the spirit of a "prehumous" obituary. In the eyes of Harriet and Sidney Janis, Duchamp was the embodiment of the "anti-artist," which is quite a remarkable assertion considering the fact that in the same paragraph they state quite positively that, despite his having turned away from art, he continued to create "new works," albeit works "so unorthodox and so far removed from (...) painting and sculpture."[99] Adopting a strictly orthodox surrealist stance, the literature and art theorist Nicolas Calas, who like Duchamp had emigrated from Paris to New York, portrayed him as the perfect revolutionary who challenged the traditional genres, ridiculed the adoration of the masterpiece, and sold to collectors and investors masterpieces "too fragile to last."[100]

The American art critic and specialist in sectarian religious movements, Robert Allerton Parker, observed in his article, "America Discovers Marcel," that Duchamp had become "a sort of subversive guru to hundreds – possibly thousands" of people in the art scene.[101] Parker was a great admirer of Duchamp. He had already interviewed him in 1915 and had put him up in his apartment in Gracie Square during the first month following his, Duchamp's, return to New York in 1942.[102] Parker could have easily substantiated his guru thesis simply by citing, before any of the other many Duchamp disciples, Charles Henri Ford and Parker Tyler, the editors of *View*, who, in dithyrambic eulogies, declaimed: "Marcel – mysterious as the internal changes of a star"[103] – "Duchamp: the chrysalis joyfully, maliciously, transcending the butterfly."[104] It would be wrong, Parker stressed, to consider Duchamp primarily as an artist, for he was "an artist only incidentally," the true key to his significance lying in his own self.[105] "His real life work has been to explore the depths of his own being, to maintain his own reality (...) he has, with subtle alchemy, transmuted the baser materials of life into the radiant myth of 'Marcel' – a masterpiece even more arresting than the *Nude Descending a Staircase*."[106] It was precisely this "radiant myth of 'Marcel'" that both the enigmatic autobiographical photomontage on the cover of *View* and the mysterious self-portrait "at the Age of 85" were meant to perpetuate.

Almost all of the contributors to the Duchamp issue of *View* sought less to embark upon an analysis of Duchamp's work than to furnish a "portrait" of Duchamp as an artistic individual and human being. They were obviously of the opinion that Duchamp's personality was either to be the focal point of attention or, if not that, then at least added to all his artistic doings and makings. Moreover, in approaching Duchamp in this way, they sought to fathom his inexplicable mystery: his break with painting, his apparent disinterest in success, his spontaneous charm and simultaneously impenetrable, incomprehensible character. These literary portraits were accompanied by paintings, photographs, and filmed images, including Man Ray's portrait painting *Rose cela vit* of 1923, which Duchamp, as evidenced by a letter to Man Ray, absolutely wanted to include in the issue of *View*,[107] as well as the portrait photograph that Man Ray had taken for the *Monte Carlo Bond*.[108]

Duchamp responded to these portrayals, which with the exception of Kiesler's photomontage *Poème espace dédié à H(ieronymous) Duchamp* all harked back to the past, with a self-portrait from the future. Here Duchamp's "little game between 'I' and 'me'" seems to make direct reference to the contributions of two of his friends. The New York authoress, Ettie Stettheimer, with whom Duchamp had been friends since his first stay in America, had contributed a short story entitled "A Portrait" under the pseudonym "Henrie Waste."[109] In this story, she reflects upon the changes that longstanding friends notice about one another when they meet up again after years of separation. The protagonist is a certain Pierre Delaire, who surprises Susanna, the character through whose eyes the story is told, with his "almost naked skull." The story is illustrated with a photo-

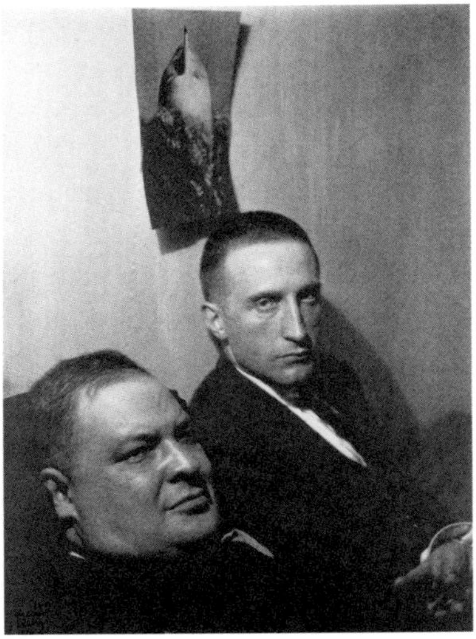

Marcel Duchamp and Joseph Stella, New York, 1920. Photo: Man Ray

graph by Man Ray, taken in New York in 1920 and showing Marcel Duchamp with short-shorn hair. Indeed, the biographical context of the story is clearly Duchamp's. Visible on the photograph, on the wall above Duchamp's head, is another photograph by Man Ray showing a woman's long, flowing mane of hair. With the loss of his hair, Delaire/Duchamp also loses his identity: "She [Susanna] thought rather that his delicate fairish classicality of a dry and cerebral quality had all of beauty except beauty's peculiar thrill. And now, his head shorn of its most vital, fluid and adventurous feature, the long fair hair he brushed firmly back – now his almost naked skull, though in itself correct enough, revealed with brutal frankness the structural bony materiality of the whole. He looked even less vitalized, less sappy than before, she thought; more rigid, more 'nature morte'. How horrible of me to think so."[110] Susanna warns him not to tell her on any account why he has cut off his hair, for "Samson, you know, lost his strength with his hair: you seem to be in danger of losing your mystery!"[111] Duchamp's self-portrait at the age of 85, apparently hairless ("almost naked skull") and awakening associations with a life or death mask ("nature morte"), seems to have evolved, at least partially, from a dialogue with Ettie Stettheimer's literary portrait. Contrary to the warning voiced by his New York friend, Duchamp's loss of hair in no way made him lose his mystery, but posed yet another puzzle for his admirers and disciples.

While Duchamp's self-portrait as an old man certainly echoes Stettheimer's short story, it responds even more directly to Breton's "Testimony 45," the opening article to the Duchamp number of *View.*[112] Having maintained in this article that Duchamp's *Large Glass* had the same significance for modern art that Kant's *Critique of Pure Reason* had for modern philosophy, Breton ventured to assert that Duchamp was "the only one of all his contemporaries who is in no way inclined to grow older."[113] Duchamp saw this far less euphorically and, at the end of all the homages and eulogies in *View,* furnished – in the form of a photograph showing how he himself would look at the age of 85 – the irrefutable proof that even he, Duchamp, was not immune to the ravages of time.

To be sure, Duchamp's response both to the well-meaning warning given by his friend Ettie and to the effusive statement of André Breton's, to whom he stood closer at that time than any other French artist or writer in New York,[114] was not without irony, and yet it was not just the dialogue with the two contributions from his friends that had prompted him to publish this self-portrait at an advanced age. Growing older had evidently become a problem for the then fifty-seven-year-old

Duchamp. He already broached the theme back in 1942, when the changing physiognomy of his female alter ego Rrose Sélavy had made him decide to publish a surrogate portrait in the exhibition catalogue *First Papers of Surrealism*, namely a close-up of the haggard face of an American farmer's wife. This photograph belonged to a series of so-called "compensation portraits," which Duchamp and Breton had cut out of books and magazines and related, either through facial similarities or other aspects, to their fellow artist celebrities.[115] Thus Matta, the youngest among the Surrealist painters in New York, was allocated the portrait of a bright youngster in a sailor suit, while André Masson made his appearance as an Eskimo and Max Ernst as an Old Testament prophet. For his own "compensation portrait," Duchamp chose a cropped image from a photograph taken by the social-documentary photographer Ben Shahn of a farmer's wife, prematurely aged through toil and deprivation, whose facial features did indeed bear a resemblance to Duchamp's own.[116] This was the last image of Rrose Sélavy to be circulated by Duchamp. She was evidently beginning to show her age and, moreover, had suffered a social decline, no longer being the elegant, seductive, and well-heeled young lady she once was. In placing a reproduction of his painting *Cemetery of Uniforms and Liveries of 1913* above this compensation portrait, Duchamp clearly associated the haggard, careworn face of the farmer's wife with death.[117]

Three years later, Duchamp finally found himself able to come to terms with what Gottfried Benn called "ageing as a problem for artists," no longer projecting it onto someone else but stepping in front of the mirror himself in the guise of an old man.[118] All the same, this glance into the future, into the last phase of his creative life, was altogether more optimistic than the surrogate portrait of Rrose Sélavy. There is nothing in

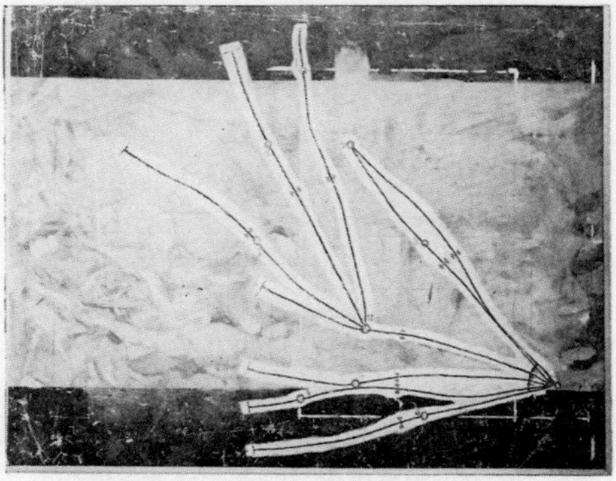

Marcel Duchamp: *Cimetière des Uniformes et Livrées* (1913)
(*Coll. Stella*)

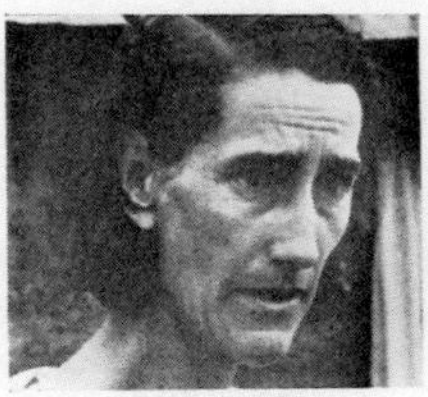

Marcel Duchamp

Page from exhibition catalogue *First Papers of Surrealism*, New York, 1945

the photograph of *Marcel Duchamp at the Age of 85* that might hint at a loss of intellectual alertness and mental agility. Duchamp imagines spending the end of his life in full possession of his mental faculties. The choice of the pose – that of the introverted thinker with downcast eyes and prominent cranium – was possibly influenced by a drawing by the New York caricaturist, Marius de Zayas, which had been published in the magazine *Camera Work* in 1912 under the title *L'accoucheur d'idées* [The Midwife of Ideas].[119] Marius was the brother of the aforementioned graphic artist, Georges de Zayas, then living in Paris, who had shaved Duchamp's comet-shaped tonsure. While the term "accoucheur d'idées" was exactly in keeping with Duchamp's understanding of himself as an artist, his fictitious self-portrait as an old man has nothing of the inner turmoil of Marius de Zayas's portrayal of the thinker. On the contrary, Duchamp casts himself, especially in the photograph without spectacles, wholly in the role of the inward-gazing artist-philosopher, entirely at one with himself.

In a letter penned at the beginning of 1946 to his clandestine lover in New York, the Brazilian sculptress Maria Martins,[120] Duchamp, who at the time was staying at the house of Mary Reynolds, his companion of the past twenty years or so, laments his mood of gloom and dwindling sexual powers: "I feel completely out of place, have not been *able* to make love, and feel more and more like ending it all."[121] Biographical sources are unable to tell us whether this was just a momentary attack of depression or a more profound state of melancholia brought on by advancing age. One bizarre anecdote, written by Hélène Hoppenot, a close friend of Mary Reynolds, in her diary of 1949, may play a significant role in this present study, for it tells how Duchamp once encountered himself as an already dead artist: "Mary told me that Marcel Duchamp was invited one

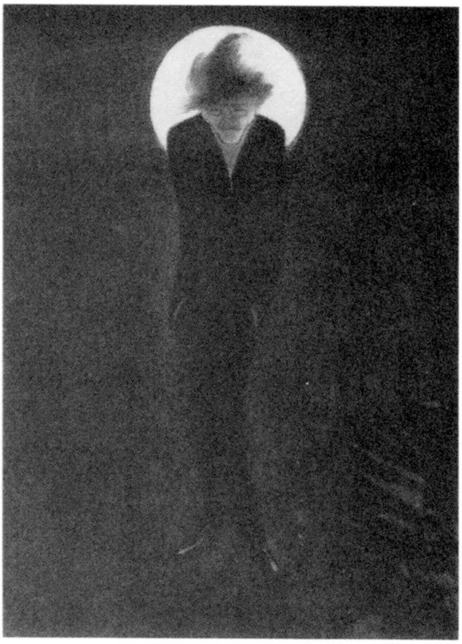

Marius de Zayas,
L'accoucheur d'idées.
From: *Camera Work*,
1912

day by the director of a municipal museum in the United States and came across a picture postcard on the sales counter illustrating one of his works. He bought it. The caption on the back of the card gave the date of his birth ... and his death!"[122] The indicated time – "one day" – does not tell us how long before 1949 this "encounter" actually took place. If it did in fact take place before January 1945, it would be yet another addition to the already complex jigsaw puzzle of experiences, feelings, and thoughts – so difficult to piece together from surviving sources – that inspired Duchamp to portray himself at the imaginary age of 85.

Photography as a time machine

Inasmuch as it claims to capture a view of the future, *Marcel Duchamp at the Age of 85* is a piece of photographic fiction. Thoughts and fantasies about life in the future are rather a matter for the literary genre of science fiction. Several clues suggest that Duchamp's familiarity with H. G. Wells's *The Time Machine* of 1895, that great classic of science fiction, went into the making of his self-portrait from the future. This novel about a voyage into the fourth dimension was published in serialized form in the French magazine *Mercure de France* in the winter of 1898–99. Alfred Jarry responded to the novel in February 1899 with an essay published in the same magazine under the title *Commentaire pour servir à la construction pratique de la machine à explorer le temps* [Commentary and Instructions for the Practical Construction of the Time Machine]. Both this essay and Jarry's *Gestes et opinions du docteur Faustroll, pataphysicien* [Exploits and Opinions of Dr. Faustroll, Pataphysician], published posthumously in 1911, had been valuable sources of inspiration for Duchamp's literary notes and preparatory sketches – later published as the so-called *Green Box* in 1934 – for *La mariée mise à nu par ses célibataires, même* [The Bride Stripped Bare By Her Bachelors, Even], better known as *Le Grand Verre* [The Large Glass]. Marc Décimo has shown how meticulously Duchamp had studied Gaston de Pawlowski's *Voyage au pays de la quatrième dimension* [Journey to the Land of the Fourth Dimension], a novel written entirely in the Wellsian tradition.[123] As a large sheaf of notes in the *White Box* shows, reflections on the visualization of four-dimensional hyperspace were central to Duchamp's conception of the *Large Glass*.[124] Taking all this into account, we may readily assume that H. G. Wells's novel *The Time Machine* cannot possibly have escaped Duchamp's attention in the course of his studies on the fourth dimension between the years of 1912 and 1915.

Wells opens the story with a heated discussion among a circle of friends, who meet once a week, about the latest theories on four-dimensional geometry. The protagonist, a scientist and inventor from Richmond, who remains nameless throughout the story and is referred to simply as the "Time Traveller," explains to his guests – a Psychologist, a Medical Man, a Provincial Mayor, and an Editor, among others – that Euclidean geometry as taught at school is no longer valid and the new geometry is based on the notion that "any real body must have extension in *four* directions: it must have Length, Breadth, Thickness, and – Duration."[125] Thus, if we wished to experience reality in its very fullness, we would have to complement the three planes of classical geometry with the dimension of time. As one of the most curious results of his preoccupation with four-dimensional geometry, the Time Traveller puts forward to this gathering of representatives of science, public opinion, and common sense the idea that the three-dimensional appearance of a human being at a given age is only a section, a kind of momentary slice of the four-dimensional being as it evolves over time. "For instance, here is a portrait of a man at eight years old, another at fifteen, another at seventeen, another at twenty-three, and so on. All these are evidently sections, as it were, Three-Dimensional representations of his Four-Dimensioned being, which is a fixed and unalterable thing."[126] If one sought to visualize this idea, the result would be either a photomontage of portraits from the various years of the subject's past life or a multiple exposure of these portraits on one single print. This would not in any way be new or exciting from an artistic standpoint. Duchamp reacts to the Time Traveller's discourse in quite a rudimentary way by juxtaposing in the *View* magazine two portraits from different phases of his life – one from 1922 and one from 1972 – and yet in so doing he addresses a far more complicated question, for the idea behind it cannot be readily visualized, at least not photographically: can one take a photograph of a person at an age not reached until some time in the future?

Advised by his sceptical interlocutors that the difference between the three classical dimensions of space and the dimension of time lay in the fact that one can move about in the various dimensions of space but not in that of time, the Time Traveller responds by presenting an "experimental verification" of his theory that such was no longer the case: the small model of a machine that, simply through the pressing of a lever, can travel through time.[127] By reason of its size – "scarcely larger than a small clock" – and the materials used in its making – "glittering brass and ivory," the model of the Time Machine must have reminded the contemporary reader, albeit only faintly, of a camera.[128] Now since a camera is an apparatus that captures moments of the present in the continual flux of time, the images it generates cannot but belong to the past. Indeed, the photograph is so closely bound up with the subject's physical existence that it must necessarily project the latter *from the past* into the viewer's present. Roland Barthes's "that-has-been" notion of photography recognizes the specific psychology of the photographic image that essentially differentiates it from the drawn or painted image.[129] However, in portraying himself at the age of 85, Duchamp contravened all photographic conventions, for his camera captured moments of the future, not of the present, entirely after the fashion of the Wellsian time machine. In so doing, Duchamp had marked the beginning of a new artistic approach to photography, that is, photography not as the documentation of a past moment but rather photography as the "documentation" of the fictional, as the visual actualization of what is yet to come, with all its truths and untruths.

Duchamp loved to think the impossible, caring little about those accepted notions of the sciences that for physiological reasons deny the human being every insight into the future and the four-dimensional time-space continuum. Exploring the boundaries of the possible had been the basic principle behind Duchamp's artistic researches and experiments since 1912. By constantly sounding out these boundaries, and indeed crossing them in defiance of all scientific certainties, Duchamp was able to extend, with almost every work, his repertoire of possible forms of artistic expression. Thus it was that with his self-portrait at the age of 85 Duchamp brought together two completely different media, the medium of photography, the very quintessence of factuality that even passes as scientific evidence before a court of law, and the medium of fiction – playacting and masquerade – as a means of creating a new, imaginary photographic self-image. Of course, Duchamp could easily have painted this self-portrait, just as the photographer Man Ray had painted *The Imaginary Portrait of the Marquis de Sade*, but painting had long since been out of the question for Duchamp by 1945 and the painting of imaginary portraits was far too conventional for him anyway. The invention of an imaginary photographic self-portrait, on the other hand, posed a new artistic challenge.

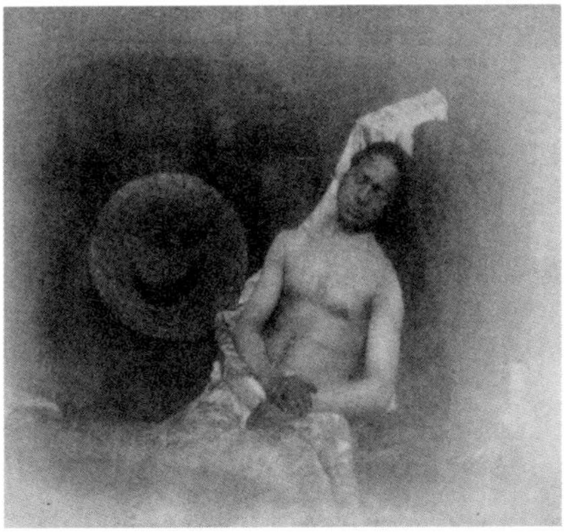

Hippolyte Bayard, *Self-Portrait as a Drowned Man*, 1840

Masquerades, cross-dressing, and absurd scenarios of every description, especially when it came to playacting and posing for staged photographs, were an immense source of fun among the Surrealists.[130] And while Breton and Duchamp had in 1942 augmented classical portraiture with a new genre, the compensation portrait, nobody had so far come up with a self-portrait from the future. The idea of photographing events that had never happened was actually nothing new. In 1840, Hippolyte Bayard, the inventor of the direct positive printing process, had circulated among the painters and actors of the Parisian Bohème a photograph of himself as a drowned man, a photograph that was in fact the first of a new genre: staged photography.[131] A long text on the back of the photograph furnished an explanation of what the photograph portrayed: the public exhibition of the corpse at the morgue following the death of the inventor who, through disappointment over the lack of recognition for his invention, had thrown himself into the Seine.[132] A monograph on Bayard was published in Paris in 1943, the plate section of which opened with his "self-portrait as a drowned man."[133] Duchamp may possibly have been familiar with this book, but his own self-portrait "at the age of 85" by far outdoes, conceptually, Bayard's fictitious self-portrait "as a drowned man." Bayard's photograph is, like any other photograph, a record of the past, for it is ostensibly a document evidencing a past suicide, albeit one that in reality did not take place. It does nothing more than exploit the potential of the camera to deceive the eye, the latter being accustomed to believing what the camera sees, namely the "that-has-been" quality of the photographic image. Duchamp's self-portrait as an old man, on the other hand, documents a journey through time into the future, into the year of 1972, when the subject will be eighty-five years of age. Thus it does not capture something that did not happen in reality but rather something that may perhaps happen in the future. It is not a photograph of what is real but of what is possible.[134]

Fictional photography and the idea of the "infra-mince"

There is another associative link between Duchamp's self-portrait at the age of 85 and Wells's novel, namely the notion of subliminal perception. Before the inventor sets off on his journey into the distant future, he demonstrates the working of the Time Machine with the aid of a small model. As soon as the latter was set in motion, the following happened: "There was a breath of wind, and the lamp flame jumped. One of the candles on the mantel was blown out, and the little machine suddenly swung round, became indistinct, was seen as a ghost for a second perhaps, as an eddy of faintly glittering brass and ivory; and it was gone – vanished! Save for the lamp the table was bare."[135] But which way did the machine go, into the past or into the future? Accounting for the disappearance of the machine, the Time Traveller speaks of "presentation below the threshold" and "diluted presentation", phenomena which, he says, could be better explained by the Psychologist than he himself: "We cannot see it," says the Psychologist, "nor can we appreciate this machine, any more than we can the spoke of a wheel spinning, or a bullet flying through the air. If it is travelling through time fifty times or a hundred times faster than we are, if it gets through a minute while we get through a second, the impression it creates will of course be only one-fiftieth or one-hundredth of what it would make if it were not travelling in time."[136] This reference to the invisible "spoke of a wheel spinning" cannot but remind us of the "Bicycle Wheel" of 1913, Duchamp's first Readymade consisting of a bicycle wheel and fork mounted upside down on a wooden stool, an object vaguely reminiscent of some makeshift experimental set-up.[137] For a whole decade, from 1935 until 1945, Duchamp had been deeply preoccupied with ultra-fine sensations experienced at the very limits of the human being's faculties of perception.[138] The notes found after his death contained a whole collection of observations and reflections on such perceptual phenomena, for which he had coined his own term: *infra-mince*, a hybrid expression combining the Latin prefix "infra" ["below"] with the French adjective "mince" ["thin", "slim", "small", "tiny"].[139] One of these notes recalls the "bullet flying through the air" from the Psychologist's explanation of the Time Machine's disappearance: "Infra thin separation between the *detonation* noise of a gun (very close) and the *apparition* of the bullet hole in the target (maximum distance 3 to 4 meters). – Shooting gallery at a fair."[140] It was on the back cover of *View* that Duchamp had published an olfactory example of ultra-fine sensory perception. This French text, which comprised a collage of different fonts and was shaped vaguely like an irregularly spreading fume of tobacco smoke, reads, in translation, as follows: "When the tobacco smoke smells also of the mouth which exhales it, the two smells marry by infra-thin," i.e., in an infinitely fine manner.[141] An arrow underneath the signature points to the right, towards the front cover, on which is depicted, against a nocturnal, starry sky, a Bordeaux bottle covered with dust and mould, out of which two puffs of smoke emerge. As we know from Kiesler's draft article and Peter Lindamood's column, "I Cover the Cover," the text of the label, illegible on account of the coarse halftone

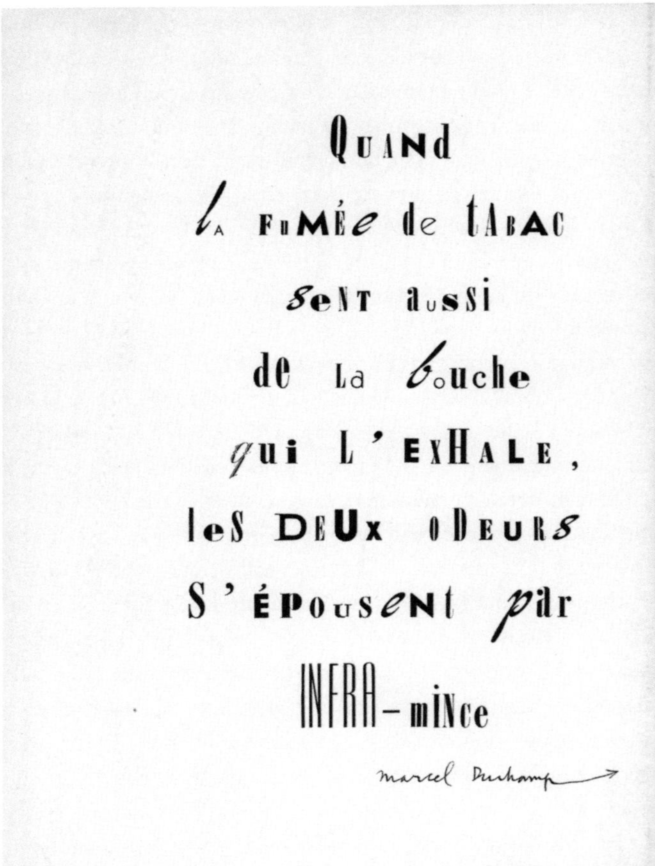

Quand
la fumée de tabac
sent aussi
de la bouche
qui l'exhale,
les deux odeurs
s'épousent par
infra-mince

Marcel Duchamp →

View, Marcel Duchamp Number, March 1945
(back cover)

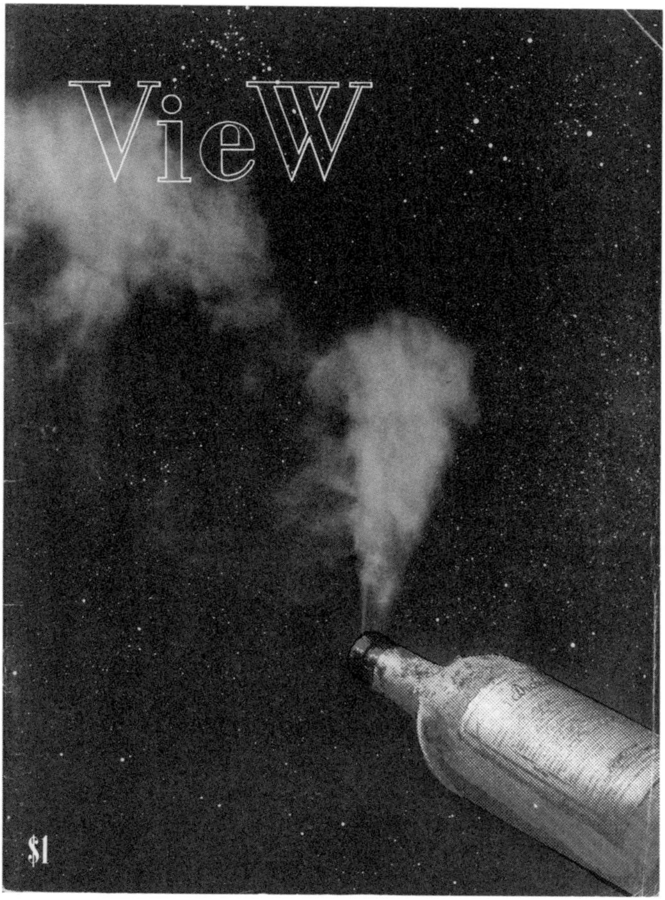

View, Marcel Duchamp Number, March 1945
(front cover)

screen used in its printing, is based on the personal particulars of Duchamp's military ID pass. The only word that can be made out, though by no means clearly, is the name "Duchamp". Bearing the traces of many years' cellaring, the bottle is evidently an ironic embodiment of Duchamp himself and/or of his work. If we are to go by Kiesler's draft article, Duchamp had had difficulty finding a genuine Bordeaux bottle in New York.[142] But it had to be such a bottle and no other, as only Bordeaux wines suffer the same fate as works of art in the course of their history: they are classified. In 1952, Duchamp wrote to his brother-in-law, the Swiss painter, Jean Crotti: "I believe in the original perfume [of the work of art], but, as all perfume, it evaporates very quickly (after a couple of weeks, or a couple of years maximum); what is left is the dried kernel classified by the art historians in the chapter 'history of art.'"[143] Here, however, it is not a dried kernel that graces the front cover of *View* but an empty, dust-encrusted wine bottle, and one that immediately awakens associations with one of Duchamp's most famous Readymades, the *Bottle Drier*. And the puffs of smoke, which also make us think of the proverbial Genii in the Bottle,[144] are the tobacco smoke that smells of the mouth *of the artist who exhales it*, a metaphor that is in no way far-fetched, for the cigar was Marcel Duchamp's most marked attribute, and he was never seen in public without it. The eccentric American painter, Laurence Vail, whom he had known since around 1937, probably inspired Duchamp's idea for his artistic transformation of a wine bottle. At the beginning of 1945, Vail had prepared an exhibition of fantastic landscapes of painted wine bottles.[145] As announced in an advertisement in the Duchamp Number of *View*, Vail's "exhibition of bottles" was to be shown in February – March of that year at the *Art of this Century*, the gallery owned by Peggy Guggenheim, Vail's ex-wife.[146] As Duchamp included his artistically prepared wine bottle in the shop window display of the Gotham Book Mart a month later, but did not seem to think it was worth preserving as an original, it is not clear whether he considered it as a work of art or merely as source material for the photomontage.

Yet another idea may have crept into the making of this enigmatic photomontage on the front cover of *View*. In May 1944, roughly half a year before the planning of the Marcel Duchamp Number, Katherine Dreier and Matta Echaurren had written a short essay on the *Large Glass*, in which they conclude: "(...) through his 'Glass' – 'La Mariée' – he causes one to realize the futility of trying to possess that which does not belong to the material world. For the moment one wants to possess and grasp at it – that moment it eludes one *and like smoke, it vanishes into thin air*" [my italics].[147] It was precisely this risk, the risk of being possessed, of being interpreted and classified by others, be they collectors, gallery owners, curators, friends or fellow artists, that Duchamp strove to oppose, both through his photomontage on the front cover of *View* and through his enigmatic self-portrait at the age of 85. Is it not more than just a coincidence that the graphic artist responsible for the layout of *View* should have placed an advertisement for Dreier's and Matta's book, *Duchamp's Glass*, next to the two Duchamp portraits at the age of 35 and 85?[148] We may readily assume that Duchamp had had a hand in this, just as with the layout and illustration of Ettie Stettheimer's short story.

Shortly after the publication of *View*, the Swiss author Denis de Rougemont asked Duchamp about the meaning of the category *infra-mince*. Replying that it would be best explained by way of examples, Duchamp continued: "It is something that escapes our scientific definitions. I expressly chose the word 'mince,' which is a human, emotive word and not a precise laboratory measure. The sound of music made by corduroy trousers rubbing together when you walk falls into the category of infra-mince. The space between the front and back of a thin sheet of paper."[149] The aesthetic of subliminal perception also underlies Duchamp's self-portrait at the age of 85. "The possible is an infra-thin. (...) the possible implying the becoming – the passage from one to the other takes place in the infra-thin," Duchamp writes in the notes found after his death.[150] It is the almost imperceptible nuances, created simply by an overly tired, "morning-after" face and a little powder and make-up, that lead the viewer to believe that he is being shown a veritable passage in time "from one to the other" and that the portrait of Duchamp, actually taken at the age of fifty-seven, is to all appearances the portrait of a very old man. Added to this, and even more important than the physiognomic nuances, is the factual assertion contained in the caption: "This is Marcel Duchamp at the age of 85." This additional use of language subliminally conditions the viewer's visual perception and points it in a certain direction of understanding. "The convention of the arrow sign produces an infra-thin reaction on the sense of displacement agreed to," Duchamp writes in another of his notes on this infinitely fine perceptual phenomenon.[151] Applying this thought of Duchamp's to the combined entity of caption and photograph, we cannot but conclude that our perception of captioned photographs is always governed by a reading action that imperceptibly steers our seeing action. Just as a vector arrow on a diagram subtly steers our thoughts about the direction of movement of the object represented in the diagram, so too does the caption of a photograph steer our perception of the depicted subject in a certain direction and towards a certain assumption, this being, in the particular case in hand, the assumption that we are actually looking at a photograph of Marcel Duchamp at a ripe old age.

The portrait caption would at first glance seem to be purely denotative: "This is Marcel Duchamp" – a factual assertion that can be easily verified through non-photographic documentary evidence and does in fact prove to be true, but the additional, qualifying words "at the age of 85" simultaneously contradict the facts. Any *View* reader familiar with the art scene of 1945 will have known that this statement of Duchamp's age was incorrect. Moreover, the year indicated above the portrait was "1972", and nobody, with the exception of dyed-in-the-wool spiritualists, could possibly have believed in photographs from the future. Thus, in combining a true and a false statement, the caption beneath Duchamp's self-portrait is at once denotative and connotative.[152] The deliberately false message – "This is a photograph from the future" – prompts us to reflect on our conventional way of perceiving the photographic image, indeed, when combined with Duchamp's staged self-portrayal rather than with a run-of-the-mill documentary photograph, it demonstrates the possibility of using photography conceptually, that is to say, not just as a mechanical means of recording factual information but also for visualizing artistic fiction.

Marcel Duchamp at the Age of 85 is a staged, fictional photograph. My use of the term "fiction" places this kind of photographic image very close to the genres of literature and poetry. Unlike the everyday and scientific use of language, the fictional use of language in a literary work does not presuppose the actual existence of the subject matter. In the discourse on the medium of photography, however, truth and reference have from the very beginning been essential categories.[153] From our knowledge of the physical conditions governing the production of the photographic image we may always assume, when looking at a photograph, the "necessarily real" existence of its referent.[154] Bound up with this assumption is the conviction that photography, being a means of depicting only what actually exists physically, is incapable of producing a mental image. "In spite of its inexhaustibility, writes Siegfried Kracauer, the photography and film theorist, "the poetic work of art is, through its form, more equivocal than a photographic message, as the latter cannot transmute the subject matter that forms its basis entirely into form."[155] Taking up the ideas of Paul Valéry, Wolfgang Preisendanz has expanded upon Kracauer's theory, remarking that since a photograph is neither shaped nor formed it is not a picture in the original sense of the word. As a photograph is only a reproduction of a given object or situation rather than the result of any intellectual activity, Preisendanz argues, it is the very opposite of "invention" and "construction," "of artistic fiction or design."[156] In the self-portrait *Marcel Duchamp at the Age of 85*, however, the rules of the conventional discourse on photography have been thwarted, for the given object here reproduced, the depicted person, is himself the result of his own thought-through and deliberate action, of his own "invention" and "construction." What here seems to be a body of plain and obvious facts – the deep, shadowy eye sockets, the unshaven, hollow cheeks, the apparent baldness, in fact the very things we perceive in ordinary portrait photographs as "pure contingence" (Roland Barthes)[157] and therefore take to be authentic – has been devised, constructed, brought about. All the photographer now had to do was to record, with his camera, this self-projection into the future – objectively, unemotionally and without any claim whatsoever to artistic merit.

Even though we know, by reason of Kiesler's draft article, that the self-portrait has been *staged*, the photograph still retains the full force of its visual evidence and, by the same token, still has a confusing effect on us, for it altogether contradicts our habitual reception of photographic images. The paradox of

Duchamp's self-portrait at the age of 85 lies in our conviction that, while we are equally convinced that photographs from the future cannot possibly exist, any object or person depicted in a photograph must have really existed. It would be too superficial of us to discuss Duchamp's self-portrait on the same level as filmic, masquerade or carnival portraiture,[158] for in aiming the camera at the future, so to speak, and disguising the physiognomic changes as the natural consequences of old age, Duchamp has camouflaged the theatrical element, which is precisely what characterizes such photographs. Moreover, the fiction resides not just in the pose and the theatrical make-up but also, and perhaps equally so, in the photographic process itself, inasmuch as the abstracting and transforming properties of black-and-white photography have been so exploited as to blur the make-up and convincingly suggest the complexion of a man in his dotage. As far as the physical representational relationship is concerned, there is little sense in arguing about the truth or untruth of a certain photograph, as the truth content can be established only in terms of the archetypal image, that is, in terms of whether this extract of reality had been found in its unchanged state or had been partially or wholly constructed. Even when the fictional and the theatrical are transported into the sphere of the factual, the photograph still cannot disclose the truth or reality of its subject matter, for – as the grammarian would say – there is no visible transition from the subjunctive to the indicative mood. This question of truth or untruth can here be verified and clarified only by non-photographic means.

Duchamp's staged self-portrait as an old man was an innovative contribution not only to the genre of the self-portrait but also to the use of photography as a medium of artistic expression. The deliberate game of confusion played by this photograph "from the future" at once presupposed and contradicted the belief in the physical existence of the photographed subject, a firmly established belief based on the law of causality and substantiated by the widespread use of photography. Duchamp used and "abused" the evidential character of photography in order to lend a figment of the imagination the appearance of physical reality. Framed by the text, "1972 – Marcel Duchamp at the Age of 85," the photographic image becomes the central piece of a complex game of visual and textual elements that shows how photography can be put in the service of the inventive, creative mind without denying its essential function as a medium of mechanical reproduction. Like his fellow Surrealists, Man Ray, Hans Bellmer, Paul Nougé, René Magritte, and Raoul Ubac, Duchamp had taken the photographic image – which for Barthes was the "emanation" and "evidence" of the real[159] – and opened it up to the world of fantasy and ambiguity: the ambiguity of gender with his self-portrait as *Rrose Sélavy* and the ambiguity of age with his *Marcel Duchamp at the Age of 85*. Another three decades were to elapse before the conceptual photographers of the 1970s finally caught on to Duchamp's example and redefined photography as the medium of the imaginary.[160]

Marcel Duchamp at the Age of 85 is the epitome of a conceptual, fictional portrait photograph as opposed to its run-of-the-mill realistic counterpart. One might indeed see it as a subversive critique of the photographic theories of Roland Barthes a good thirty years before the latter were written. Barthes defines photography in terms of its factual evidentiality, the "that-has-been" aspect of the photographic image being the very essence of the medium.[161] "[Photography] does not invent," writes Barthes in his *Camera Lucida*, "[it is] impotent with regard to general ideas (fiction)"[162] and can never be anything but "an emanation of past reality."[163] Here Barthes excludes from his definition of photography all staged, fictional practices, notwithstanding the fact such practices had from the very beginning been just as valid an aspect of photography as its documentary and factual categories. Duchamp's self-portrait at the fictitious age of 85 proves that photography is a process that is not only subject to physical laws but also follows cultural conventions that may indeed be brushed against the grain. By guiding the viewer's imagination not into the past but into the future, not into the finite realm of "past reality" but into the infinite realm of the possible, towards, in other words, happenings that have not yet occurred, Duchamp shows how and to what extent the photographic image can indeed be used for "invention." That the subject of a photograph can also have a metaphorical presence is demonstrated not least by the two variants of the self-portrait at the age of 85, the one depicting an old man of ordinary appearance, the other the calm physiognomy of a philosopher engrossed in deep thought. Jean Cocteau once remarked on Duchamp as the "inventor of that unreal realism that will be the mark of the 20th century."[164] It was a remark that reflected exactly the paradox behind the fictional portrait of Duchamp as an old man, for it transports our faculty of perception far beyond the factual into the unreal spaces of the imagination. And the fiction is indeed infinite: the Marcel Duchamp shown in this photograph at the age of 85 will never be able to die, for in real life he did not live to that age. He died on October 2, 1968 at the age of 81 years.

NOTES

1 *View*, Marcel Duchamp Number, p. 18: *Counter-Art-Wise Duchamp, arch rebel of 20th century art, stopped painting more than twenty years ago. Nevertheless, new works continue to come into being (…). These works are scarcely recognizable as the products of creative activity: they are so unorthodox and so far removed from patterns, centuries-old, of the material and conceptual substance of painting and sculpture.*

2 On Duchamp as a graphic artist see Bonk, Britt (eds.): *Marcel Duchamp. The Box in a Valise;* Naumann: *Marcel Duchamp: The Art of Making Art; Marcel Duchamp Druckgraphik*, exh. cat., Vienna.

3 "Peut-on faire des œuvres qui ne soient pas d'art?" First published in: Marcel Duchamp: *A l' Infinitif.* Quoted here, in translation, from: Sanouillet (ed.), *Duchamp du Signe,* p. 105.

4 This unusually small format was not an invention of Duchamp's but rather one of the magazine's stylistic layout devices that ideally suited Duchamp's purposes. It had already been used in previous issues, especially for the depiction of portraits. See, for example, *View,* vol. IV, no. 4, December 1944, pp. 118 and 121.

5 The portrait taken by Stieglitz actually dates from 1923. See Collins Goodyear, McManus (eds.), *Inventing Marcel Duchamp,* p. 164.

6 Schwarz, cat. nos. 511, 781; Taylor: *Marcel Duchamp Étant donnés,* exh. cat., pp. 53–54; Filipovic (ed.), *Marcel Duchamp,* exh. cat. Fundación Proa, Buenos Aires, pp. 246–47. A comparison of the size of the displayed photograph with that of the immediately adjacent book *Surrealism* by Julien Levy shows that its dimensions were approximately the same as those of the two surviving original prints (17 × 11.6 cm and

16.8 × 11.9 cm). – From the original photographs of the shop window, which are kept in the collection of the Bibliothèque Kandinsky of the Centre Georges Pompidou in Paris, it is not possible to make out whether the displayed photograph is the one taken with spectacles or the other version, without spectacles, which is yet to be discussed below.

7 See *View*, vol. V, no. 2, May 1945, p. 41: The *View* editors named the window display "*LAZY HARDWARE": Duchamp – View – Arcane 17 window*. Displayed besides the original photograph was an opened copy of the Marcel Duchamp Number of *View* itself and the orignial Bordeaux bottle as prepared by Duchamp for the production of the magazine cover. See also: Schwarz: *The Complete Works*, p. 781.

8 D'Harnoncourt, McShine (eds.), *Marcel Duchamp*, exh. cat., Museum of Modern Art, New York; Philadelphia Museum of Art, p. 24.

9 *Marcel Duchamp: Briefe an Marcel Jean / Lettres à Marcel Jean / Letters to Marcel Jean*, pp. 9, 27; Franklin: "Smoking Bottles," pp. 204–242.

10 Information given to the author by Marcel Jean, Paris, 1987. The reproduction of Stieglitz's portrait (18.7 × 18 cm on 24 × 18 cm format paper) – now in a private collection – is captioned on the back in Marcel Jean's handwriting: "Marcel Duchamp, v. 1923, d'après photo A. Stieglitz."

11 Marcel Jean, *Histoire de la peinture surréaliste*, p. 352. The photograph is wrongly dated in the caption to 1947. The illustration is also contained in the English (*The History of Surrealist Painting*, p. 352) and the German (*Geschichte des Surrealismus*, p. 352) editions of the book.

12 16.8 × 11.9 cm. Written in pencil on the back, probably in Duchamp's own handwriting, are the words: "photo faite en NY 1946" (sic). Also written on the back, in unknown handwriting, are a page reference "Page 352" (this is the page on which the photograph is illustrated in Marcel Jean's *Histoire de la peinture surréaliste*) and an indication of size "55 mm" for the platemaker.

13 *Marcel Duchamp*, exh. cat. Ronny van de Velde Gallery; the work was here reproduced as a picture postcard.

14 Schwarz, *The Complete Works*, p. 780, cat. no. 509.

15 Ibid.

16 Molderings, "Die Fotografie des Möglichen,"p. 458; idem, *Die Moderne der Fotografie*, p. 109; exh. cat. *Marcel Duchamp*, p. 22.

17 *Durs Grünbein im Gespräch mit Heinz-Norbert Jocks*, p. 27. Exhibited as a facsimile in: *Rollenspiele – Rollenbilder*, exh. cat. Museum der Moderne Salzburg, p. 102 and *Evan Penny Refigured*, exh. cat., Kunsthalle Tübingen, Museum der Moderne Salzburg, Art Gallery of Toronto, p.153.

18 Hopkins, "The Politics of Equivocation," p. 55. Like Schwarz, the author wrongly assumes that the portrait is the one published in *View* (p. 56). See also Molderings, Wedekind: *L'évidence photographique: La conception positiviste de la photographie en question*, p. 205; Molderings: *L'évidence du possible. Photographie moderne et surrealisme*, p. 148.

19 *Inventing Marcel Duchamp*, pp. 196–197.

20 Marcadé, *Marcel Duchamp. La vie à crédit*, p. 373.

21 Housez, *Marcel Duchamp*, p. 423.

22 Taylor, *Marcel Duchamp Étant donnés*, pp. 61–62.

23 Taylor, "Marcel Duchamp and Portraiture," in: *Inventing Marcel Duchamp*, p. 119.

24 Ibid., p. 61.

25 Gough-Cooper, Caumont, "Kiesler und 'die Braut, von ihren Junggesellen nackt entblößt, sogar'," p. 288; Luyken, *Frederick J. Kiesler und Marcel Duchamp: Rekonstruktion ihres theoretischen und künstlerischen Austausches von 1925 bis 1937*, pp. 30–31.

26 Kiesler, "Design-Correlation. Marcel Duchamp's 'Big Glass'," reprinted in *Frederick J. Kiesler, Selected Writings*, pp. 38–41.

27 *Affect[t] Marcel. The Selected Correspondence of Marcel Duchamp*, pp. 214–15; Luyken: *Frederick Kiesler und Marcel Duchamp*, pp. 138–39, 188–89.

28 See Landis, *Critiquing Absolutism*; Daniels, "Points d'interférence entre Frederick Kiesler et Marcel Duchamp"; Bottero, *Frederick Kiesler*, pp. 212 et passim; Taylor, *Marcel Duchamp Étant donnés*, pp. 48–64. – Following a particularly intensive collaboration in 1947 – see Molderings: *Die nackte Wahrheit*, pp. 139 et passim – Duchamp broke off relations with Kiesler in 1948 probably in consequence of the "Matta affair" following the suicide of Arshile Gorky. Tomkins, *Marcel Duchamp*, p. 424.

29 Davidson, Rylands (eds.), *Peggy Guggenheim & Frederick Kiesler*, pp. 258–59.

30 *VVV*. Almanac for 1943, nos. 2–3, March 1943, p. 144 and back cover.

31 See *VVV*, 1 and back cover as well as Duchamp's original design, in: Schwarz: *The Complete Works*, p. 769, cat. no. 491; also Bonk, Britt (eds.): *Marcel Duchamp. The Box in a Valise*, pp. 280–81.

32 On Duchamp's reflections on "inframince" phenomena see Davila, *De l'inframince;* von Graevenitz, "Duchamp as a Scientist, Artifex, and Semiotic Philosopher"; Semin, "Note sur l'*inframince* duchampien,; Clements, "Duchamp's Infrathin," pp. 70–90; Nesbit, "Last Words (Rilke, Wittgenstein) (Duchamp)"; Tono, "Duchamp und 'Inframince'."

33 Bogner, *Friedrich Kiesler 1890–1965*, pp. 58–65; Landis, "Critiquing Absolutism," pp. 126–28; Phillips, "Architect of Endless Innovation," in: idem, *Frederick Kiesler*, pp. 26–27.

34 *Ephemerides on and about Marcel Duchamp and Rrose Sélavy*, December 22, [1944].

35 On December 24, 1944, Duchamp wrote to Man Ray, who was then living in Los Angeles, informing him of the planned "Duchamp number" in *View* and asking him to send him documentary material on the artistic activities they had jointly undertaken. *Affect*[t] *Marcel. The Selected Correspondence*, p. 247.

36 Letter dated August 21, 1945. Quoted, in translation, from: Scarlett and Philippe Reliquet (eds.), *Correspondance Marcel Duchamp – Henri-Pierre Roché 1918–1959*, p. 70: *J'ai réussi à vivre ici presque comme à Paris càd. en évitant la vie publique*

(expositions, cocktails, parties) – Malgré cela j'ai dû aider à la confection d'un N° de "View" (...).

37 *View*, pp. 25–29. On Kiesler's theory of "Correalism" see Kiesler: "Manifeste du Correalisme," Paris, 1947, reprinted in: Bogner, *Friedrich Kiesler 1890–1965*, pp. 92–121.

38 For detailed interpretations of this photomontage cf. Otwell, *View* magazine's *Marcel Duchamp Special Issue*, chapter 3, http://www.heyotwell.com/work/arthistory/thesis/intro.html; Kraus, Sonzogni, "Frederick Kiesler: 'Les Larves d'Imagie d'Henri Robert Marcel Duchamp,'' pp. 82–88; Dalrymple Henderson, *Duchamp in Context*, pp. 214–15. Taylor, *Marcel Duchamp Étant donnés*, pp. 62–65.

39 *View*, no. 25, pp. 29–30.

40 Kiesler's typescript, folio 1: "This was the first of 11 photographs that the 2 of us, he and I, had taken of Duchamp and his studio 2 days previously on the 4th floor of the house at 210 W 14 Str.; folio 2: [I] stood up and, after taking about five steps, was (...) looking, for the very first time, at the photographs he and I had taken. Folio 6: I sat down at the table, gathered my 11 prints together and began to pack them into my briefcase."

41 *Art Digest*, vol. II, no. 7, January 1, 1937, p. 31. I am indebted to Paul Franklin for this information.

42 See the reproduction of the painting *Sad Young Man on a Train* (1942) in the Alexina and Marcel Duchamp Papers, Series X–A, Box 22, Folder no. 56, Philadelphia Museum of Art. On the dating of the reproduction cf. Franklin, "Smoking Bottles," p. 235. – Rainford is also credited as a photographer in Robert Lebel's monograph *Sur Marcel Duchamp*, p. 155, but without the photographs being specified.

43 See Kiesler, *Inside The Endless House*, p. 194. Here Kiesler is mistaken about the years of publication of *VVV*. The magazine was not published in 1947 but from 1942 until 1944, in three issues.

44 Cf. entry in Stefi Kiesler's desk diary of January 1, 1945: *2 h (Rainford – Marcel)*. Austrian Lillian and Frederick Kiesler Private Archive, Vienna.

45 Ibid. In his diary entry dated March 10, 1959, Kiesler estimates Rainford's age at "about fifty". The photographer might therefore have been the same Percy Rainford who, according to the US Social Security Death Index, was born on November 9, 1901 and died in September 1976 (Bronx, New York). While these are the dates probably referred to by Michael R. Taylor in *Marcel Duchamp Étant donnés,* p. 62, there is still no documentary evidence to the effect that the two Percy Rainfords are one and the same.

46 Kiesler's typescript, folio 1: "He then went over to the young Negro;" folio 2: "The assistant appeared with a dripping print (…)."

47 Kiesler: *Inside the Endless House,* p. 194.

48 Kiesler's typescript, folios 1 and 2.

49 Ibid., folio 2.

50 Kiesler: *Inside the Endless House,* p. 195.

51 Kiesler's typescript, folio 6.

52 See "Quick Prints from Wet Negatives," in: Encyclopedia of Photography, New York, 1974, p. 447. – That the negatives and prints had been developed in great haste is proven by the many fine drying spots on both prints, which indicate the presence of residual moisture on the films as a result of inadequate drying. If Rainford did in fact use glass plates instead of sheet film – which is not known for certain – he could have made the contact prints from wet negatives, which would have speeded up the production process by as much as about twenty minutes.

53 Of the portrait without spectacles there exists in the collection of the Philadelphia Museum of Art a second, unsuccessful print, which is damaged on its left-hand edge and incomplete along its bottom edge. *Inventing Marcel Duchamp,* p. 197, Plate 44.

54 Kiesler's typescript, folio 7. As there was no such thing as instant photography in those days, the prints could not possibly have been ready in just a "few minutes." Kiesler has evidently speeded up the happenings for the sake of the narrative.

55 Kiesler, *Inside the Endless House*, p. 195.

56 Kiesler's typescript, folio 3.

57 Ibid., folio 4.

58 Kiesler's typescript, folio 9.

59 Ibid., folio 10.

60 *Marcel Duchamp Notes*, p. 107 (Note 174): *Catalogue – Épisodaire / Page de titre – reproduction 1re page livret militaire – / par années – déplacements et tableaux faits dans l'année / pour ceux qui ne sont pas reproduits dans la boîte peut être indiquer non-reproduit / Ceci pour le luxe seulement 10 ou 50 exemplaires.*

61 In his essay "Smoking Bottles" (p. 234), Paul B. Franklin suggests an interpretation of this note in connection with Duchamp's work on the *Boîte-en-Valise* [The Box in a Valise] between the years of 1935 and 1941. However, as the photograph of the first page of Duchamp's military ID pass was made later, during preparations for the Duchamp issue of *View*, we may readily assume that the photograph rather documents a later rejected project for the limited edition of this magazine. Indeed, when it was finally realized, the limited edition of a hundred copies of *View* featured on its frontispiece, as a rectified readymade, a hand-colored and signed reproduction of the print *Pharmacy* (1914). See Bonk, Britt: *Marcel Duchamp. The Box in a Valise*, p. 168.

62 Letter from Duchamp to Henri-Pierre Roché dated November 26, 1953: "Please find enclosed the cover for the brochure you asked me for. The first page of my military ID card: a photo I found in my papers. Use it as it is, including the much-thumbed corners, on a white (or colored) background (...)," in: *Correspondance Duchamp – Roché*, p. 172. Quoted in translation. Two prints of this photograph were found in Duchamp's estate and now belong to the Alexina and Marcel Duchamp Papers in the archives of the Philadelphia Museum of Art. See Franklin, "Smoking Bottles," p. 233. – One print from the estate of André Breton was auctioned in 2003 in a joint lot together with the Marcel Duchamp Number of *View*. Auction catalogue *André Breton*, Livres I, no. 519.

63 The photographer can be readily identified as Percy Rainford with the aid of the entries in Stefi Kiesler's diary dated January 1 and 11, 1945 (Austrian Frederick and Lillian Kiesler Private Foundation). See Gough-Cooper, Caumont, "Kiesler und die Braut ...," p. 292; Kraus, Sonzogni, "Frederick Kiesler: Les Larves d'Imagie d'Henri Robert Marcel Duchamp," p. 83.

64 It might have been footage from Maya Deren's film *The Witch's Cradle* (1943). A strip of film comprising 10 frames showing the movement of a camera around Duchamp's head is illustrated in *View*, no. 34. However, as Duchamp had in 1943 also been making short films of his *Rotoreliefs* in movement, it is just as possible that this roll of film had been taken from one of these films. See also *Affect[t] Marcel*, p. 236.

65 *View*, no. 3. – On Peter Lindamood see *From Blues to Haikus: An Interview with Charles Henri Ford*, n.p. [4] and Franklin, "Smoking Bottles," pp. 234–235.

66 *From Blues to Haikus*, n.p. [4]

67 Ibid., n.p. [3].

68 *View*, vol. IV, no. 4, December 1944.

69 *View*, vol. VI, no. 2, May 1946.

70 As Kiesler has here invented a French word (*Imagie*), the title can only be translated approximately.

71 Kiesler's typescript, folio 9.

72 Kiesler's typescript, folio 1. The number of the house – 42 – is either a typing or a memory error on Kiesler's part. In Rainford's advertisement in *Art Digest* of 1937 (see note 41) his address reads 44 West 57th Street. In the Manhattan New York City Telephone Directory of 1940 and Fall–Winter 1946 the studio "Percy Rainford Photography" is listed under the address "44 W 57" and telephone number CIrcle-7-3983.

73 Ibid., folio 2. Duchamp's words "I must look like 84" were deleted by Kiesler in the typescript.

74 Ibid., folio 3.

75 Ibid., folios 4 and 5.

76 According to Kiesler's typescript the photographer took two photographs of each pose. See folio 5.

77 Ibid., folio 4.

78 Ibid., folio 7.

79 Ibid.

80 The aesthetic closeness of the portrait to a face mask is certainly not fortuitous. Back in 1941, the sculptor Georges Henriques Raba in Sanary-sur-Mer had modelled a face mask of Duchamp and used it for the making of a portrait in colored cement. From 1946 onwards, Duchamp's work was essentially marked by the technique of lifecasting. This phase ended, significantly, with a self-portrait that operates with the aesthetic of a life mask: *With my Tongue in my Cheek*, 1959. See Franklin: "Rencontres à Sanary-sur-Mer," pp. 278–279; Didi-Huberman, *Ähnlichkeit und Berührung*, chapter III, pp. 108–189; Taylor, "Marcel Duchamp and Portraiture," pp. 117–121; idem, *Marcel Duchamp Étant donnés*, pp. 61–62; Judovitz, *Unpacking Duchamp: Art in Transit*, pp. 116–117.

81 Katherine Kuh, "Marcel Duchamp," in: idem, *The Artist's Voice*, p. 83.

82 *Inventing Marcel Duchamp*, p. 137; MacManus, "Trucage photographique," pp. 94–111; Blunck, "Chimären im Spiegel," pp. 3–14.

83 Chaplot, *La photographie récréative*, pp. 37–41.

84 Barthes, *Camera lucida*, p. 21.

85 Quoted, in translation, from: Fritz Franz Vogel, *The Cindy Shermans: inszenierte Identitäten*, p. 204.

86 Lebel, *Sur Marcel Duchamp*, p. 98, caption to fig. 26: *Marcel Duchamp: étoile rasée par Georges de Zayas*, Paris, 1921; Franklin, "Portfolio: Photographs of or about Marcel Duchamp," pp. 221–223.

87 *Ephemerides on and about Marcel Duchamp and Rrose Sélavy*, November 1, 1921.

88 Franklin: "Portfolio: Photographs of or about Marcel Duchamp," pp. 221–223.

89 Duchamp to Alexander Liberman (1960). Quoted, in translation, from: Liberman, *Les Maîtres de l'art contemporain*, p. 57: *La vie d'un artiste est comparable à celle d'un moine, d'un moine laïque si vous voulez, et même d'un moine très rabelaisien. Mais ce n'est ni plus ni moins qu'une ordination.*

90 Sanouillet, Peterson (eds.), *Salt Seller: The Writings of Marcel Duchamp*, p. 26.

91 On one of the "tonsure" portraits Duchamp later wrote: *Voici rrose sélavy 1921.* (This is Rrose Sélavy 1921). See *Inventing Marcel Duchamp*, p. 159.

92 Giovanna Zapperi associates Duchamp's "tonsure" portrait with the ideological notion of the priest of art. Zapperi, "Marcel Duchamp's Tonsure," pp. 294–298.

93 Schwarz: *The Complete Works*, p. 703, cat. no. 406.

94 Ades, "Duchamp's Masquerades," pp. 94–114; Roth, *Difference/Indifference*, pp. 14–30. Roth interprets Duchamp's role plays within the context of his self-presentation as a dandy. The self-portrait of "Duchamp at the Age of 85" is mentioned in neither of these essays.

95 Quoted from: Kuenzli, Naumann (eds.), *Marcel Duchamp. Artist of the Century*, p. 19.

96 *Inventing Duchamp*, p. 196. – Between 1893 and 1912, Alphonse Bertillon, who systematized mugshot photography, also used this technique for the taking of self-portraits. See *Le Photographe photographié. L'autoportrait en France 1850–1914*, exhib. cat., Paris musées, Maison Européenne de la Photographie, 2004, p. 50.

97 *Inventing Duchamp*, Plate 65.

98 Ibid., p. 196.

99 Harriet and Sidney Janis, "Marcel Duchamp Anti-Artist," *View*, no. 18. Theses of the same tenor are also to be found in Sidney Janis's book *Abstract & Surrealist Art in America*,

which had been published a few months previously and was discussed in detail in the Marcel Duchamp Number of *View.* Ibid., pp. 39–40. See also the half-page advertisement, ibid., p. 42. – On the aesthetic consequences of Duchamp's "perte du métier" see: Didi-Huberman, *La Ressemblance par contact,* chapter entitled *Formes critiques.*

100 Calas, "Cheat to Cheat," *View,* p. 20. On Calas's collaboration with *View* see Franklin, "Smoking Bottles," p. 231.

101 Parker, "America Discovers Marcel," *View,* p. 33.

102 Tomkins, *Marcel Duchamp,* p. 384.

103 *View,* p. 37.

104 Ibid.

105 Ibid., p. 33.

106 Ibid., p. 51.

107 *View,* p. 35. – Letter from Duchamp to Man Ray dated 12/24/1944: "Can you send any documents (photographic or other) retracing our relationship over the last thirty years (…). For example, do you have a photo of your portrait of Rrose Sélavy?" *Affect[t] Marcel,* p. 247.

108 *View,* p. 32. Dated here to 1925.

109 *View,* pp. 34–35.

110 *View,* p. 35.

111 Ibid.

112 Naumann: *Marcel Duchamp. The Art of Making Art,* p. 161. The title "Testimony 45" probably refers to the difficulties experienced by French immigrants in obtaining the necessary documents for settlement in the USA. See Hopkins, "The Politics of Equivocation," pp. 57–58.

113 *View,* p. 5.

114 On December 17, 1944 Duchamp wrote to Henri-Pierre Roché in Paris: "Breton est le seul que je voie assez souvent". See *Correspondance Duchamp – Roché,* p. 67.

115 This technique was later adopted and varied, in 1996, by the French artist and writer Édouard Levé. See Édouard Levé: "Homonymes," in: *Les Cahiers du Musée national d'art moderne,* no. 84, 2003, pp. 3–13.

116 See entire photograph in Hopkins, "The Politics of Equivocation," p. 56. On the social and political implications of Duchamp's choice of photograph see: ibid, pp. 56–57.

117 The painting is normally titled *Réseaux des stoppages-étalon* [Networks of Stoppages]. Schwarz, *The Complete Works,* p. 607, cat. no. 292. It was under this title that Duchamp had reproduced it only shortly before in his *Boîte-en-valise.* Cf. Bonk, *Marcel Duchamp. The Box in a Valise,* p. 54. Thus it is all the more remarkable that, simply through a different title (Cemetery of Uniforms and Liveries), it should here be associated with death.

118 Benn: *Altern als Problem für Künstler.*

119 Naumann (ed.), *How, When, And Why Modern Art Came To New York,* p. 78.

120 On the importance of Maria Martins in Marcel Duchamp's life between the years of 1945 and 1951 see Naumann, "Marcel and Maria," pp. 102–105; Taylor: *Marcel Duchamp Étant donnés,* pp. 26–32; Molderings: *Die nackte Wahrheit,* op. cit., pp. 85–87, 130–133.

121 Taylor: *Marcel Duchamp Étant donnés,* op. cit., p. 404, letter dated May 12, 1946: "Je suis complètement dépaysé, n'ai pas <u>pu</u> faire l'amour et j'ai de plus en plus envie de disparaître."

122 See Franklin: "Mary Reynolds et Hélène Hoppenot. Confidences," in: *Étant donné Marcel Duchamp,* pp. 134–35, entry dated December 30, 1949: "Mary me dit que Marcel Duchamp fut invité un jour par le conservateur d'un musée d'une ville des États-Unis et qu'il aperçut au stand de vente une carte postale reproduisant une de ses œuvres. Il l'acheta. Au dos, elle portait la date de sa naissance … et de sa mort!"

123 Décimo, *La bibliothèque de Marcel Duchamp,* pp. 20 et passim.

124 See Henderson, *Duchamp in Context;* Molderings, "Ästhetik des Möglichen …," pp. 103–135; idem, *Kunst als Experiment;*

Adcock, *Marcel Duchamp's Notes from the Large Glass: An N-Dimensional Analysis.*

125 H. G. Wells, *The Time Machine.* Here quoted from: H. G. Wells, *The Time Machine.* Bartleby.com, 2000. www.bartleby.com/1000/. [11/15/2012], chapter 1.

126 Ibid.

127 Ibid.

128 Ibid.

129 Barthes: *Camera Lucida,* p. 77 et passim.

130 Molderings, "Evidenz des Möglichen. Fotografie und Surrealismus," in: idem, *Moderne der Fotografie,* pp. 93–154; *La Subversion des images. Surréalisme Photographie Film,* exh. cat., Musée national d'art moderne, Centre Georges Pompidou, Paris.

131 Vogel, *The Cindy Shermans: Inszenierte Identitäten,* pp. 40–41.

132 Schaaf, "Wahre Künstler sterben gern!" pp. 33–37; Komninou, "Hippolyte Bayard's *Le Noyé,*" pp. 163–170; Sapir, "The Impossible Photograph: Hippolyte Bayard's *Self-Portrait as a Drowned Man,*" pp. 619–629; Keeler, "Souvenirs of the Invention of Photography on Paper, pp. 47–62.

133 Lo Duca: *Bayard,* Plates I and II.

134 Molderings, "Die Fotografie des Möglichen,"; idem, "Evidenz des Möglichen. Fotografie und Surrealismus," pp. 105–121.

135 Wells: *The Time Machine,* chapter 1.

136 Ibid.

137 On the significance of Wells's novel for Duchamp's *Bicycle Wheel* see Dee: "Ce façonnement symétrique," p. 365; Molderings, "Ästhetik des Möglichen," pp. 124–125.

138 On the aesthetic of the "infra-mince" see Semin: "Note sur l'*inframince* duchampien"; Davila, *De l'inframince*; von Graevenitz, "Duchamp as a Scientist," op. cit.

139 In Duchamp's Notes this term is spelt in different ways: *inframince, infra-mince* and *infra mince.* See *Marcel Duchamp Notes,* pp. 20–35.

140 Ibid., p. 24. The original French text reads: *Séparation infra mince entre le bruit de detonation d'un fusil (très proche) et l'apparition de la marque de la balle sur la cible (distance maximum 3 à 4 mètres. – Tir de foire).*

141 *Quand la fumée de tabac sent aussi de la bouche qui l'exhale, les deux odeurs s'épousent par infra-mince.* This sentence, in duplicate and in a slightly changed form, forms part of the 46 notes written by Duchamp between 1935 and 1945 on the subject of "infra-mince". See *Marcel Duchamp Notes*, pp. 24 and 33.

142 Kiesler's typescript, folio 8. – According to Lindamood's "I Cover the Cover" the Bordeaux bottle was a left-over from an evening when Duchamp and Breton had dined together. *View*, p. 3.

143 *Affect[t] Marcel*, p. 320.

144 Zaunschirm, *Marcel Duchamps Unbekanntes Meisterwerk*, p. 113.

145 Tomkins: *Marcel Duchamp*, p. 367.

146 *View*, p. 42.

147 Dreier, Echaurren, *Duchamp's Glass*, n.p.

148 *View*, p. 53.

149 Quoted, in translation, from: De Rougemont, "Marcel Duchamp mine de rien," pp. 46–47. *C'est quelque chose qui échappe à nos définitions scientifiques. J'ai pris à dessein le mot mince qui est un mot humain, affectif, et non pas une mesure précise de laboratoire. Le bruit ou la musique que fait un pantalon de velours côtelé comme celui-ci, quand on bouge, relève de l'infra-mince. Le creux dans le papier, entre le recto et le verso d'une feuille mince …* In this interview Duchamp associates, like the Psychologist in H.G. Wells's novel, subliminal perception with the dimension theory: *Je crois que par l'infra-mince on peut passer de la deuxième à la troisième dimension* (*I believe that through the infra-mince it is possible to pass from the second to the third dimension*).

150 *Marcel Duchamp Notes*, 21: *Le possible est un infra mince. (...) Le possible impliquant le devenir – le passage de l'un à l'autre a lieu dans l'infra mince.*

151 Ibid., p. 22: *La convention du signe de la flèche produit une réaction infra mince sur le sens de déplacement accepté.*

152 On the difference between a denotative and a connotative caption see: Preisendanz, "Verordnete Wahrnehmung," pp. 2–4. See also: John Elsom (ed.), *Is Shakespeare Still Our Contemporary*, p. 35.

153 Stiegler, *Theoriegeschichte der Photographie*, chapter 7.1: Zwischen Trauma und Emanation des Referenten: Roland Barthes, pp. 341–349.

154 Barthes, *Camera Lucida*, p. 76.

155 Quoted, in translation, from: Preisendanz, "Verordnete Wahrnehmung," p. 2.

156 Ibid., p. 2. On the Valéry reference see chapter: Valéry, *Gedanken*, p. 7.

157 Barthes, *Camera Lucida*, p. 28.

158 On theatrical role portraiture see Vogel, *The Cindy Shermans*, pp. 30–31.

159 Barthes, *Camera Lucida*, pp. 88 and 107.

160 Molderings, "Evidenz des Möglichen," pp. 135–144; Foucault, "La pensée, l'émotion" (1982), p. 1062; Quoi: *Histoire(s) du Narrative Art (1965–1981).*

161 Barthes, *Camera Lucida*, pp. 77 et passim.

162 Ibid., p. 87.

163 Ibid., p. 88.

164 Quoted, in translation, from: Gervais, "33 lettres et cartes à Robert Lebel (1955–1960) au sujet de *Sur Marcel Duchamp*," in: *Les Cahiers du Musée national d'art moderne*, no. 84, 2003, p. 49, note 82.

Bibliography

Adcock, Craig E.: *Marcel Duchamp's Notes from the Large Glass: An N-Dimensional Analysis,* UMI, Ann Arbor, Mich., 1983.

Ades, Dawn: "Duchamp's Masquerades", in: Graham Clarke (ed.): *The Portrait in Photography*, Reaktion books, London, 1992, pp. 94–114.

Barthes, Roland. *Camera lucida: Reflections on photography*, transl. by R. Howard, Hill & Wang, New York, 1981.

Benn, Gottfried: *Altern als Problem für Künstler*, Limes, Wiesbaden, 1954.

Blunck, Lars: "Chimären im Spiegel. Anmerkungen zur sogenannten Multifotografie". *Fotogeschichte*, vol. 94, 2004–05, pp. 3–14.

Bogner, Dieter: *Friedrich Kiesler 1890–1965. Inside The Endless House (Begleitbuch der 231. Sonderausstellung des Historischen Museums der Stadt Wien).* Böhlau, Vienna, 1997.

Bogner, Dieter (ed.): *Friedrich Kiesler Architekt Maler Bildhauer 1890–1965*, Löcker, Vienna, 1988.

Bonk, Ecke: *Marcel Duchamp. The Box in a Valise*, New York: Rizzoli, 1989.

Bottero, Maria: *Frederick Kiesler. Arte, Architettura, Ambiente*, Milan 1995.

Chaplot, Charles: *La photographie récréative et fantaisiste,* Charles Mendel, Paris, 1904.

Clements, Cal: "Duchamp's Infrathin". In: *Pataphysica,* Lincoln, NE 2002, pp. 70–90.

Davidson, Susan, Rylands, Philip (eds.): *Peggy Guggenheim & Frederick Kiesler. The Story of Art of This Century*, Guggenheim Museum Publications, New York, 2004.

Davila, Thierry: *De l'inframince. Brève histoire de l'imperceptible, de Marcel Duchamp à nos jours*, Éditions du regard, Paris, 2010.

Décimo, Marc: *La bibliothèque de Marcel Duchamp, peut-être*, les presses du réel, Dijon, 2002.

Dee, John: "Ce façonnement symétrique", in: *Duchamp. Colloque de Cerisy*, Union générale d'éditions, Paris, 1979, pp. 351–397.

De Rougemont, Denis: "Marcel Duchamp mine de rien", in *Preuves*, Paris, vol. XVIII, no. 204, February 1968, pp. 43–47.

Didi-Huberman, Georges, *La Ressemblance par contact – Archéologie, anachronisme et modernité de l'empreinte*, Les Éditions de Minuit, Collection "Paradox", Paris, 2008.

Dreier, Katherine S., Matta Echaurren: *Duchamp's Glass. La Mariée mise à nu par ses célibataires, même. An Analytical Reflection.* Société Anonyme, New York, 1944.

Marcel Duchamp. Duchamp du Signe. Écrits, ed. by Michel Sanouillet, Flammarion, Paris, 1975.

— *Affect[t] Marcel. The Selected Correspondence of Marcel Duchamp*, ed. by Francis M. Naumann and Hector Obalk, Thames & Hudson, London, 2000.

— *Ephemerides on and about Marcel Duchamp and Rrose Sélavy*, by Jennifer Gough-Cooper and Jacques Caumont. In: Pontus Hulten (ed.) *Marcel Duchamp Work and Life*, Thames & Hudson, London; The MIT Press, Cambridge, Mass., 1993, n. p.

— *Inventing Marcel Duchamp: The Dynamics of Portraiture*, ed. by Anne Collins Goodyear, James W. McManus, The MIT Press, Cambridge, Mass./London, 2009.

— M. Sanouillet and E. Peterson eds., *Salt Seller: The Writings of Marcel Duchamp (Marchand du sel)*, Da Capo, New York, 1973.

— *Marcel Duchamp. Interviews und Statements.* Gesammelt, übersetzt und annotiert von Serge Stauffer, Hatje Cantz, Ostfildern-Ruit, 1992.

— *Marcel Duchamp. Briefe an Marcel Jean / Lettres à Marcel Jean / Letters to Marcel Jean*, Silke Schreiber, Munich, 1987.

— *L'œuvre de Marcel Duchamp*, exh. cat., Musée National d'art moderne, Centre Georges Pompidou, Paris, 1977.

— *Marcel Duchamp*, exh. cat., The Museum of Modern Art; New York and the Philadelphia Museum of Art, edited by Anne d'Harnoncourt and Kynaston McShine, New York, 1973.

— *Marcel Duchamp*, exh. cat., Ronny van de Velde Gallery, Antwerp, 1991.

— *Marcel Duchamp, Notes.* Foreword by Paul Matisse – Preface by Pontus Hulten, Flammarion, Paris, 1999.

— *Marcel Duchamp*, published by Museum Jean Tinguely Basel, Hatje Cantz, Ostfildern-Ruit, 2002.

— *Marcel Duchamp Druckgraphik*, exh. cat., Universität für Angewandte Kunst, Vienna, 2003.

— *Marcel Duchamp. Une obra que no es una obra "de arte"*, exh. cat., edited by Elena Filipovic, Fundación Proa, Buenos Aires, 2008.

Durs Grünbein im Gespräch mit Heinz-Norbert Jocks, DuMont, Cologne, 2001.

Elsom, John (ed.), *Is Shakespeare Still Our Contemporary*, Routledge, London/ New York, 1989.

Evan Penny Refigured, exh. cat., Kunsthalle Tübingen, Museum der Moderne Salzburg, Art Gallery of Toronto, MARCA, Catanzaro, Cologne, 2011.

First Papers of Surrealism. Hanging by André Breton / his twine Marcel Duchamp, exh. cat., Coordinating Council of French Relief Societies, New York, 1942.

Foucault, Michel, "La pensée, l'émotion" (1982), in: *Dits et écrits*, vol. II, 1976–1988, Gallimard, Paris, 2001.

Franklin, Paul B., "Smoking Bottles," in: *Étant donné Marcel Duchamp*, no. 10, 2011, pp. 204–242.

— "Portfolio: Photographs of or about Marcel Duchamp", in: *Étant donné Marcel Duchamp*, no. 7, 2006, pp. 221–223.

— "Rencontres à Sanary-sur-Mer" in *Étant donné Marcel Duchamp*, no. 10, 2011, pp. 258–289.

— "Mary Reynolds et Hélène Hoppenot. Confidences: un dialogue à travers les lettres de Mary Reynolds et le journal intime d'Hélène Hoppenot", in *: Étant donné Marcel Duchamp*, no. 8, 2007, pp. 106–145.

"From Blues to Haikus: An Interview with Charles Henri Ford", in: *tout-fait. The Marcel Duchamp Studies online journal*, 2, May 2000.

Gervais, André: "33 lettres et cartes à Robert Lebel (1955–1960) au sujet de *Sur Marcel Duchamp*", in: *Les Cahiers du Musée national d'art moderne*, no. 84, 2003, pp. 14–47.

Gough-Cooper, Caumont:"Kiesler und die 'Braut, von ihren Junggesellen nackt entblößt, sogar'", in: Bogner, Dieter (ed.), *Friedrich Kiesler. Architekt Maler Bildhauer 1890–1965*, Löcker, Vienna, 1988, pp. 286–296.

Graevenitz, Antje von: "Duchamp as a Scientist, Artifex, and Semiotic Philosopher", in: Banz, Stefan (ed.): *Marcel Duchamp and the Forestay Waterfall*, jrp ringier, Zurich, 2010, pp. 216–231.

Henderson, Linda Dalrymple: *Duchamp in Context. Science and Technology in the 'Large Glass' and Related Works*, Princeton University Press, Princeton, 1998.

Hopkins, David: "The Politics of Equivocation: Sherrie Levine, Duchamp's 'Compensation Portrait' , and Surrealism in the USA 1942–45". *The Oxford Art Journal*, vol. XXVI, no. 1, 2003, pp. 45–68.

Housez, Judith: *Marcel Duchamp. Biographie*, Grasset, Paris, 2006.

Ich ist etwas Anderes. Kunst am Ende des 20. Jahrhunderts, exh. cat., Kunstsammlung Nordrhein-Westfalen, Düsseldorf 2000.

Janis, Sidney: *Abstract & Surrealist Art in America*, Reynal & Hitchcock, New York, 1944.

Jean, Marcel: *Histoire de la peinture surréaliste*, du Sueil, Paris, 1959.

Jones, B.E. (ed), *The Encyclopedia of Photography*, Arno, New York, 1974.

Judovitz, Dalia. *Unpacking Duchamp: Art in Transit.* University of California Press, Berkeley, 1995.

Keeler, Nancy: "Souvenirs of the Invention of Photography on Paper: Bayard, Talbot, and the Triumph of Negative-Positive-Photography", in: *Photography: Discovery and Invention*, The J. Paul Getty Museum, Los Angeles, 1990, pp. 47–62.

Kiesler, Frederick J.: "Design-Correlation. Marcel Duchamp's 'Big Glass'". *Architectural Record*, no. 5, May 1937, pp. 53–60.

Kiesler, Frederick J.: *Inside the Endless House*, Simon & Schuster, New York, 1966.

Kiesler, Frederick J. Selected Writing. Edited by Siegfried Gohr and Gunda Luyken, Gerd Hatje, Ostfildern/Stuttgart, 1996.

Frederick Kiesler. Artiste-architecte, exh. cat., Musée national d'art moderne, Centre Georges Pompidou, Paris, 1996.

Komninou, Effie: "Hippolyte Bayard's *Le Noyé*: A Little Meditation on Death", in: *Third Text*, no. 2, 2003, pp. 163–170.

Kraus, Eva Christina, Sonzogni, Valentina: "Frederick Kiesler: 'Les Larves d'Imagie d'Henri Robert Marcel Duchamp", in: Kraus, Zeiller (eds.), *Marcel Duchamp Druckgraphik*, exh. cat., Universität für Angewandte Kunst, Vienna 2003, pp. 82–88.

Kuenzli, Rudolf E., Naumann, Francis M. (eds.): *Marcel Duchamp. Artist of the Century*, The MIT Press, Cambridge, Mass., 1996.

Kuh, Katharine: "Marcel Duchamp". In: idem: *The Artist's Voice. Talks with Seventeen Artists.* Harper & Row, New York and Evanston, 1962, pp. 81–93.

Landis, Linda Louise: "Critiquing Absolutism: Marcel Duchamp's *Etant donnés* and the Psychology of Perception", Dissertation Yale University 1991, UMI, 1994.

La Subversion des images. Surréalisme Photographie Film, exhib. cat., Musée national d'art moderne, Centre Georges Pompidou, Paris, 2009.

Lebel, Robert: *Sur Marcel Duchamp*, Trianon, Paris, 1959.

Le Photographe photographié. L'autoportrait en France 1850–1914, exh. cat., Paris musées, Maison Europénne de la Photographie, Paris, 2004.

Julien Levy: *Surrealism*, The Black Sunn Press, New York, 1936.

Liberman, Alexander: *Les Maîtres de l'art contemporain*, Arthaud, Paris, 1961.

Lo Duca: *Bayard*, Prisma, Paris, 1943.

Luyken, Gunda: *Frederick Kiesler und Marcel Duchamp: Rekonstruktion ihres theoretischen und künstlerischen Austausches von 1925 bis 1937*, dissertation, Staatliche Hochschule für Gestaltung, Karlsruhe, 2002.

— "Infra-geringe Verschiebungen. Beobachtungen zu den künstlerischen Konzepten von Marcel Duchamp und Frederick Kiesler", in: Antonia Napp, Kornelia Röder (eds): *Impuls Marcel Duchamp // Where Do We Go From Here?*, Hatje-Cantz, Ostfildern, 2011, pp. 128–155.

MacManus, James W.: "Trucage photographique et déplacement de l'objet : à propos d'une photographie de Marcel Duchamp prise devant un miroir à charnières (1917)". *Les Cahiers du musée national d'art moderne*, no. 92, Summer 2005, pp. 94–111.

Marcadé, Bernard: *Marcel Duchamp. La vie à crédit*, Flammarion, Paris, 2007.

Molderings, Herbert: "Die Fotografie des Möglichen. Von Marcel Duchamp bis Anna und Bernhard Blume", in: *Jahrbuch 13 der Bayerischen Akademie der Schönen Künste*, Munich, 1999, pp. 443–493.

— "Mögliche Welten. Konzeptuelle Fotografie von Marcel Duchamp bis Anna und Bernhard Blume", in: *Das Ende des 20. Jahrhunderts. Standpunkte zur Kunst in Deutschland*, edited by Joachim Jäger and Peter-Klaus Schuster, DuMont, Cologne, 2000, pp. 243–265.

— "Ästhetik des Möglichen. Zur Erfindungsgeschichte der Readymades Marcel Duchamps", in: Gert Mattenklott (ed.): *Ästhetische Erfahrung im Zeichen der Entgrenzung der Künste*,

Sonderheft des Jahrgangs 2004 der *Zeitschrift für Ästhetik und Allgemeine Kunstwissenschaft*, Hamburg, 2004, pp. 103–135.

— *Kunst als Experiment. Marcel Duchamps "3 Kunststopf-Normalmaße"*, Munich and Berlin: Deutscher Kunstverlag, 2006 / English edition: *Duchamp and the Aesthetics of Chance: Art as Experiment*, transl. John Brogden, Columbia University Press, New York, 2010.

— *Die Moderne der Fotografie*, Philo Fine Arts, Hamburg, 2008.

— *L'évidence du possible. Photographie moderne et surréalisme*, textuel, Paris, 2009.

— *Die nackte Wahrheit. Zum Spätwerk von Marcel Duchamp*, Hanser, Munich, 2012.

Molderings, Herbert, Wedekind, Gregor (eds.): *L'évidence photographique. La conception positiviste de la photographie en question*, Éditions de la Maison des sciences de l'homme, Paris, 2009.

Naumann, Francis M.: *Marcel Duchamp. The Art of Making Art in the Age of Mechanical Reproduction*, Abrams, New York, 1999.

Naumann, Francis M. (ed.): *How, When, And Why Modern Art Came To New York. Marius de Zayas*, The MIT Press, London/ Cambridge, Mass., 1996.

— "Marcel and Maria", in: *Art in America*, no. 4, 2001, pp. 102–105.

Nesbit, Molly: "Last Words (Rilke, Wittgenstein) (Duchamp)". In: *Art History*, vol. 21, no. 4, December 1998, pp. 546–564.

Otwell, Andrew: *View Magazine's Marcel Duchamp Special Issue, March 1945*, Master thesis 1997: http://www.heyotwell.com/ work/arthistory/thesis/intro.html.

Preisendanz, Wolfgang: "Verordnete Wahrnehmung. Zum Verhältnis von Photo und Begleittext" [1969], in: *Sprache im technischen Zeitalter*, edited by Walter Höllerer, no. 37, 1971, pp. 1–8.

Quoi, Alexandre: *Histoire(s) du Narrative Art (1965–1981)*. Récits photoconceptuels et formes hybrides du médium photo-texte, unpublished dissertation, Université de Paris-Sorbonne-Paris IV 2011.

Reliquet, Scarlett and Philippe (eds.), *Correspondance Marcel Duchamp – Henri-Pierre Roché 1918–1959*, MAMCO, Geneva, 2012.

Roth, Moira: *Difference/Indifference: Musings on Postmodernism, Marcel Duchamp and John Cage*, G+B Arts International, Amsterdam, 1998, pp. 14–30.

Rougemont, Denis de: "Marcel Duchamp mine de rien", Preuves, no. 204, February 1968, pp. 43–47.

Sapir, Michael: "The Impossible Photograph: Hippolyte Bayard's *Self-Portrait as a Drowned Man*", in: *Modern Fiction Studies*, no. 3, 1994, pp. 619–629.

Schaaf, Larry J.: "Wahre Künstler sterben gern!". Hippolyte Bayards 'Autoportrait en Noyé'. In: Bodo von Dewitz (ed.): *La Bohème. Die Inszenierung des Künstlers in Fotografien des 19. und 20. Jahrhunderts,* Steidl, Göttingen, 2010, pp. 33–37.

Schwarz, Arturo: *The Complete Works of Marcel Duchamp*, Delano Greenidge, New York, 1997.

Semin, Didier: "Note sur l'*inframince* duchampien, affleurement de l'intelligible dans le sensible", in: idem.: *La Piste du hérisson*, J. Chambon, Nîmes, 2004, pp. 242–247.

Stiegler, Bernd: *Theoriegeschichte der Photographie*, Wilhelm Fink, Munich, 2006.

Stooss, Toni, and Ruelfs, Esther (eds.): *Rollenspiele – Rollenbilder*, exh. cat., Museum der Moderne Salzburg, Hirmer, Munich, 2011.

Taylor, Michael R.: *Marcel Duchamp Étant donnés*, Philadelphia Museum of Art, Philadelphia, 2009.

The Definitively Unfinished Marcel Duchamp, edited by Thierry de Duve, The MIT Press, Cambridge, Mass., 1991.

Tomkins, Calvin: *Marcel Duchamp. A Biography*, Henry Holt and Company, New York, 1996.

Tono, Yoshiaki: "Duchamp und 'Inframince'". In: *Duchamp*, exh. cat. Museum Ludwig, Cologne 1984, pp. 55–58.

View, Marcel Duchamp Number, series V, no. 1, New York, March 1945.

Vogel, Fritz Franz: *The Cindy Shermans: inszenierte Identitäten. Fotogeschichten von 1840 bis 2005*, Böhlau, Cologne/Weimar/Vienna, 2006.

Wells, H. G., The Time Machine, An Invention, first published in 1898. Here quoted from: Wells, H. G. *The Time Machine.* Bartleby.com, 2000. www.bartleby.com/1000/. [15.11.2012].

Zapperi, Giovanna: "Marcel Duchamp's *Tonsure*: Towards an alternate masculinity". *Oxford Art Journal*, no. 30, 2007, pp. 289–303.

Zaunschirm, Thomas: *Marcel Duchamps Unbekanntes Meisterwerk*, Ritter, Klagenfurt, 1986.

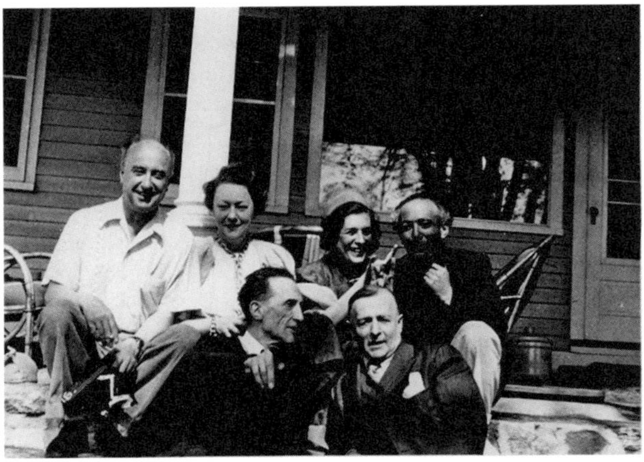

Yves Tanguy, Kay Sage, Maria Martins, Enrico Donati (back row), Marcel Duchamp and Frederick Kiesler (front row) in front of Kay Sage's house in Woodbury, Connecticut, circa 1946–47.

“I was waiting for Marcel – it was 5.35 p.m. at 42 West 57 Str., January 13, 1945.”

FREDERICK KIESLER

Editor’s note

The typescript kept under inventory no. TXT 6170/0 at the archive of the Austrian Frederick and Lillian Kiesler Private Foundation, Vienna, consists of ten loose, one-sided typewritten, paginated folios measuring 27.8 × 21.4 cm. It is neither dated nor signed. By reason of certain particulars given in the text, the correctness of which is verifiable by other documents, the script can be ascribed to Frederick (Friedrich) Kiesler beyond all shadow of doubt. It is the draft of an article intended for publication in the “Marcel Duchamp Number” of the avant-garde magazine View: The Modern Magazine *and was probably written between January 13 and March 1945, but was not published. For an in-depth commentary on the authorship and content of this draft please refer to the essay in this publication entitled “Marcel Duchamp at the Age of 85: An Incunabulum of Conceptual Photography.”*

The frequency of deletions and substitutions in the typescript suggests that the article was written directly into the typewriter. In the second stage, which consisted in the editing of the text with pencil, certain typographical and punctuation errors were corrected, words and parts of sentences deleted and replaced by others, and some sentences were transferred to other parts in the text. The article is composed in a spoken rather than written style, which not only explains a certain negligence of expression but also gives reason to assume that the text was dictated to a second person who typed it. The German of the original typescript is peculiar. It is not literary German but rather the colloquial German of an Austrian who grew up in the Jewish community of Czernowitz in the easternmost part of the then Austro-Hungarian Empire, studied and worked in Vienna and then, from the mid-1920s, lived in the USA. The linguistic mix that came about through Kiesler's many changes of abode is strongly reflected in the original German typescript. The opening sentence, written in English, and the occasional use of English words in the German text ("appropriately", "screen") are a direct echo of the fact that Kiesler had been living in New York since 1926. As the article was intended for publication in the American magazine View: The Modern Magazine, *it would still have to have been translated, but no English version of the article has so far been located or proved to have existed.*

H. M.

Translator's note

While the translation is an accurate rendering of the content, no attempt has been made – nor would it have been desirable or even feasible – to render the text in an equally peculiar English. Words and passages deleted by the author in the original typescript are indicated in the endnotes. There are two kinds of deletions: words that have been x'ed out while the text was still in the typewriter and words that have been deleted in pencil after removal from the typewriter. The deletions specified in the endnotes have been distinguished accordingly.

The paragraph divisions of the original typescript have been retained. Any additions made by the editor or the translator for the sake of clarity have been set between square brackets.

[fol. 1] I was waiting for Marcel – it was 5.35 p.m. at 42 West 57 Str., January 13, 1945.[1]

The photographer came out from behind the curtain,[2] holding[3] some wet photographs in his hand. A young Negro was lighting gas burners inside a drum, around which ran a double belt of canvas.[4] The photographer put the wet photographs, which were clogged together, on the table in front of me. He then went over to the young Negro and showed him the lever that set the drum in motion. The canvas belt began to run around the drum and from there under a metal tank, which looked like an open rain gutter, passing through a slot in the table, then around a mobile framework that articulated to and fro, continuing[5] before disappearing and then coming into view again on the other side of the drum.[6] The photographer took 3, 4 steps,[7] grabbed hold of a clean, white cloth, crumpled it up, detached the top photograph from the wet clump, laid it flat down on the table and[8] wiped it rapidly and energetically front and back with the cloth in order to soak up as much water as possible. This was the first of 11[9] photographs that the 2 of us[10] had taken of Duchamp and his studio 2 days previously on the 4th floor of the house at 210 W 14 Str.[11, 12] The photographer took hold of one of the corners of the 1st print and peeled it off the table, took it across to the machine and laid it on the bed of the rotary canvas dryer [fol. 2] and then went back for the next one, repeating the to-ing and fro-ing until all the prints [were] thus bedded and had disappeared into the toasting machine. At that very moment, I heard the door open and Marcel was in the room. His hair was grey. He looked ill. "Marcel, are you[13] all right?" "I have to[14] look even worse,"[15] he answered. He had[16] [taken] out of his pocket[17] 1 powder compact, 1 eyeliner pencil, 1 clean and neatly folded handkerchief, 1 pair of gold-rimmed spectacles, and a beret. Now I understood. He had come to have his portrait taken at the age of 84. The photographer was standing in front of the machine and, like a midwife,[18] waiting for the dried prints[19] to emerge. Marcel took off his coat, asked for a room with a mirror and disappeared down the hallway. The photographer[20] was now cutting the prints to size. [I] stood up and, after taking about five steps, was standing next to him and looking, for the very first time, at the photographs he and I had taken. One of the prints was still lying on the table, slightly rolled up, only half dry. I recognized the bottle[21] that I [had seen] at Marcel's a fortnight ago, the one he had prepared for the photography sitting. Marcel appeared. His hair was whiter, his eyebrows as white as snow, his unshaven chin grey. He pointed to his tie, a[22] black, self-tied one, 1900 style. He gave a broad, thin-lipped laugh and struck a pose, his mouth imitating that of a toothless old man. He asked for the photograph of the bottle.[23] It was shown to him. Two other prints were brought in. He wished to know which one was deeper black, asking me, and then the photographer and then the boy. Another man emerged from the darkroom. Marcel gave him the 1st print: [fol. 3] "Can you change this black into a sepia?" "Easy," he replied, disappearing behind the black curtain. "You'll have to help me finish my make-up." I accompanied Marcel into the other room, which looked like a cave, unfurnished except for a roller blind that hung down askew, an iron bedstead with a blue blanket and a large mirror on the wall, illuminated by a naked electric light, in front of which Marcel was already standing. We studied his face in the mirror for a few seconds and then another few seconds later we were back in the room. Marcel sat broadly in the chair; his head leant back, as though he were at the barber's. I grabbed the white handkerchief, wiped those parts of his hair and face that were too white and dusted the white powder off his black tie. Both of us agreed that the patches of grey on the black tie were very apt and suitable. "I have just bought the tie,[24] it's new." A few black lines across his brow, a deepening of the nasolabial folds, which Marcel had already deepened slightly, a powdering of the ears, which we had forgotten, thin black lines on both edges of the nose[25] and at the end of the nasal cartilage. Meanwhile the photographer had set up the lamps and switched them on.[26] He was now putting up a roll of white paper in the background; Marcel interrupted him – and me in my make-up work – and asked for a black background. The photographer and I looked at Marcel in his shirt, his pale face, his black beret [fol. 4] and black tie and considered him ready. Marcel wished to put on his dark jacket, as he feared he might be too easily recognizable in his shirt. The boy brought the jacket. Marcel[27] stood up, put on the jacket, took [a] few steps towards the light and sat down on a chair in front of the black background.[28] He was grinning like a very old man. I went over to him with the handkerchief, the black pencil and the powder compact and checked everything one more time. The photographer was already behind the camera under the focusing cloth. Marcel insisted that the light must come from high up so as to make the shadows[29] in the face sharp. The ceiling lamp, which created this effect quite naturally, could not be used, as it was too weak. In order to obtain the same effect, somebody would have to hold up the artificial lighting while the photograph was being taken. The assistant was called, the boy also came in, and the 2 of them raised the lamps. I stepped back, but still managed in a fleeting moment to pull down the collar of Marcel's jacket at the back in order to accentuate even more the sunken sitting posture. Marcel asked for the spectacles. I took them from the table, placed them on his ears and nose, letting them slide slightly down the ridge of his nose. "Not too low," Marcel insisted. I noticed that the lenses of the spectacles were[30] smeared and powdered (Marcel had evidently already prepared them in his studio). Marcel struck his grinning pose once more,[31] but begged me to keep a close watch on the[32] sunken lines around the mouth, as he would now widen and narrow them. I was to decide what was[33] not too wide and not too [fol. 5] narrow for an old man of 84. The photographer, still under his focusing cloth, called to me, voicing his enthusiasm about what he could see. I came and looked through [the camera].[34] The 2 assistants[35] were still holding up the lamps. I stepped back. Marcel remained motionless, frozen [in his pose]. The photographer released the shutter, changed the dark-slide and released the shutter again. Without moving his head, Marcel asked me to remove his spectacles. I did so. "The question is whether 84 would come out better with or without glasses." The camera clicked another two times. "Can you develop that straight away?" "Certainly." The photographer pulled out the dark-slide and was already passing through the curtain when Marcel, still seated, called to him: "Put your hand in my coat pocket.[36] It's hanging over there. There's a small roll of film in it." The photographer brought forth the roll of film. Marcel stood up, took the roll of film into his hand and said to the photographer, "It is only so long,"[37] and spread his arms apart, "about 7 foot.[38] I'd like you to make prints from it, simple contact prints. You may cut the film into short pieces if you like, so they will fit into your bath, I don't mind." "Oh, no," the photographer replied, "I can do it without cutting it," and disappeared behind the black curtain. The camera now stood unattended, the lamps had been placed on the floor, everybody was waiting for the test prints. The assistant appeared with a dripping print of the bottle.[39] Marcel and I stood in the light of the ceiling lamp and scrutinized the wet print, which stayed stuck[40] to the palm of the assistant's hand. [fol. 6] The tonal transformation had been successful. The print was now a golden brown. "Excellent," Duchamp said loudly and[41] turned towards the table on which the 2 other black prints of the bottle were lying. The assistant ignited the drying drum and began[42] the process of drying the prints. Marcel[43] spread the two prints out flat and held them close to my face, one in each hand. "Which print," he said, "is the darker one? This is very important. It's for the enlargement for printing." They were astonishingly equal in shade. I chose one, Marcel chose the other. The[44] photographer[45] appeared from behind the curtain and lit a cigarette. Marcel held the two prints towards him. "Which one is darker?" he asked without taking his eyes off the prints. The photographer chose the 2nd one. I had lost. The assistant, who was now standing next to us at the machine, stretched out his[46] hands towards the drum. The print dropped into his hand. He brought it over to us and then withdrew. Marcel[47] dashed through the hallway into the [other] room, saying: "I've got to be downtown at[48] 7 o'clock." The photographer disappeared behind the curtain.[49] I sat down at the table, gathered my 11 prints together and began to pack them into my briefcase.[50] He came back. "But first I must go home, 14th Street, to brush the powder out of my hair and to shave off the beard I've been growing for the last 3 days." He began to stuff his beret, powder compact, and the other props into his pocket. "There are 72 images on this 7-foot [fol. 7] roll of film," he said, smiling cheerfully through his hoary, mask-like make-up. "Printing one image from the film on each page will give a moving image when you flip through the pages. You must leave me a small space on two of your pages, about 1 to 2 cm square."[51] There was a movement behind the curtain and out came the photographer, laughing, the palms of his 2 hands holding towards us 2 dripping prints of the photographs he had taken a few minutes before.[52] Marcel with and without glasses. We bent down over them. "Which one shall we use? The one with glasses looks like 84, the one without only like 79." "May I take them with me?" Marcel asked the photographer, who then stepped to one side and ignited the drying machine. Marcel had already put on his overcoat, and I mine. He took the brown print, which was still lying on the table, into his hand and was about to put it in the envelope he was holding.[53] I looked at the bottle.[54] "Marcel," I said, "I remember how you prepared the bottle; it was about 3 weeks ago, when I visited you in your studio in order to check some of the known dates from your life.[55] On your work table was a large sheet of paper with a small pile of dust in the middle,[56] lit by an overhanging desk lamp. On the same sheet of paper was a thick piece of cardboard, about 1 foot by [fol. 8] 2, which had been scraped hollow all over. For hours and days on end you had probably been scraping away at the cardboard with a knife or some similar implement in order to produce[57] a whole mass of dust, which you then gathered up into a pile.[58] You then brought a bottle from out of the table's shadow and told me that it had been rather difficult to find a genuine Bordeaux bottle, but now you had managed to do so and were happy about it. You explained that the cardboard dust[59] had been made for the purpose of mixing it with a slightly sticky solution to make a pulp, with which the glass of the bottle would then be coated. When it had dried slightly, the pulp would then have to be scraped off the bottle, but only lightly, only so much that the dark glass would just shine through the thin layer of dust and the scratches. You then asked me whether I considered one spot that had already been prepared in this way, after the application of several layers of dust, better than another spot, which was still a pulpy clump, with cracks and fissures, like dried-out mud. I found this spot more expressive than the other for your presumed purpose, namely to make the bottle look antiquated and to fake decades of cellaring. You liked the other side of the bottle. You then turned the bottle round to show a long, stuck-on label and asked me, smiling somewhat, where the label came from. It was written in fine handwriting and in small print and looked like a document, indecipherable except for your name, which [fol. 9] stood at the top in large letters. To my great astonishment I saw that you have two other first names, Henri and Robert, and remarked happily that I was very glad that your name has an H in it. You asked me why, and I said that I myself had given you the name of Hyronymus [sic] and could therefore retain the H without any fakery.[60] It was, you now explained, a photograph[61] which you had appropriately[62] treated with diluted lacquer and light shades of color and stuck on [the bottle] as a label. It is a reproduction of your certificate of discharge from the French army of the First World War.[63] You then explained the smoke effect you wished to obtain from the neck of the bottle, the natural sunshine that would be necessary in order to create the cloud effect.[64] But what now interests me in particular is that you were intent on photographing the whole bottle again and then making a tiny 2 centimetre square block so as to obtain an image with a coarse [halftone] screen.[65] You said you would then have a print made from the tiny block, enlarge it to this magazine's format of 7 by 10,[66] making the reproduction of the bottle dissolve into large, heavy dots through the enlarged screen. You would then overprint it with the same bottle in a fine screen in 2 other colors and in this way obtain an interesting texture. [fol. 10] Now I see from this brown print that[67] the entire text of the label has been lost, not only because of the coarse screen but also because you did not photograph the bottle upright but laid almost flat and foreshortened, making it impossible to read the label. As they are unfortunately illegible on the bottle, may I now ask your permission to reproduce in this article the personal particulars of your military document, which are on the bottle and at all events give reason to assume appropriate credibility." "But of course," Marcel replied. And here is the document:

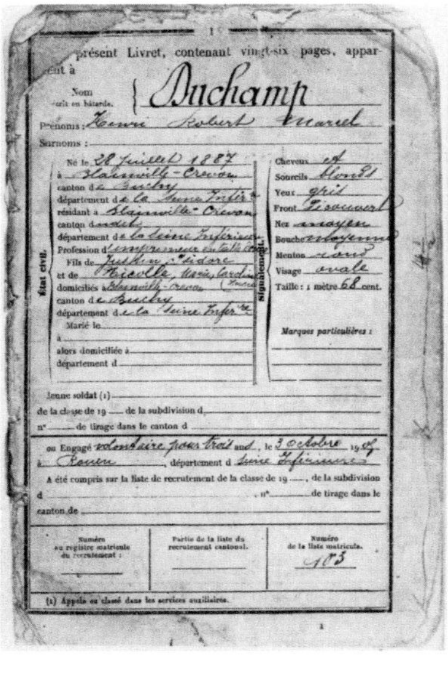
1
présent Livret, contenant vingt-six pages, appar-
tient à
Nom écrit en bâtarde. Duchamp
Prénoms : Henri Robert Marcel
Surnoms :
État civil.
Né le 28 juillet 1887
à Blainville-Crevon
canton de Buchy
département de la Seine Infér.re
résidant à Blainville-Crevon
canton d
département de la Seine Inférieure
Profession d
Fils de Justin Isidore
et de Nicolle, Marie Caroline
domiciliés à Blainville-Crevon
canton de Buchy
département de la Seine Infér.re
Marié le
à
alors domiciliée à
département d
Signalement.
Cheveux
Sourcils blonds
Yeux gris
Front
Nez moyen
Bouche moyenne
Menton rond
Visage ovale
Taille : 1 mètre 68 cent.
Marques particulières :
Jeune soldat (1)
de la classe de 19 — de la subdivision d
n° — de tirage dans le canton d
ou Engagé volontaire pour trois ans, le 3 octobre 1905
à Rouen, département d Seine Inférieure
A été compris sur la liste de recrutement de la classe de 19 —, de la subdivision
d — n° — de tirage dans le
canton de
Numéro au registre matricule du recrutement :
Partie de la liste du recrutement cantonal.
Numéro de la liste matricule. 183
(1) Appelé ou classé dans les services auxiliaires.
1

Personal particulars from Duchamp's military ID pass of 1905

NOTES

1 The title of the original German text is written in English. With the aid of the entries in Stefi Kiesler's diary dated January 1 and 11, 1945 (Austrian Frederick and Lillian Kiesler Private Foundation), the photographer can be readily identified as Percy Rainford. The number of the house – 42 – is either a typing or a memory error on Kiesler's part. The studio was located not at 42 but at 44 West 57th Street. See note 72 of the essay "Marcel Duchamp at the Age of 85" in this book.

2 *said,* x'ed out on typewriter.

3 *11,* x'ed out on typewriter.

4 *and [...] himself,* x'ed out on typewriter.

5 *and,* x'ed out on typewriter.

6 Pencilled arrow denoting continuation of paragraph.

7 *to his table,* x'ed out on typewriter.

8 *carefully pressed,* x'ed out on typewriter.

9 *prints,* x'ed out on typewriter.

10 *he and I,* x'ed out on typewriter.

11 According to the entry in Stefi Kiesler's calendar diary, the photographer Percy Rainford had, under Frederick Kiesler's instructions, taken photographs of Marcel Duchamp's single-room apartment at 210 West 14th Street on January 11, 1945. Having previously lived with the Kieslers as a lodger for a year, Duchamp had moved into this studio apartment in the autumn of 1943. He kept this room until 1965, but used it just as a studio from 1954 onwards.

12 *The first print wiped dry,* x'ed out on typewriter.

13 *ill? I asked him,* deleted in pencil.

14 *am going to,* deleted in pencil.

15 *"I must look like 84",* deleted in pencil.

16 *already,* deleted in pencil.

17 *one,* deleted in pencil.

18 Here Kiesler uses the word *accoucheur,* the French word for obstetrician. The English equivalent of the feminine form, *accoucheuse,* meaning midwife, has been used here as a more suitable translation.

19 Here Kiesler uses the German word *Kopien* (copies), which at that time was a common technical term for photographic prints.

20 *Placed the prints in a machine and cut,* deleted in pencil.

21 More about this further on in the text.

22 *kind of,* x'ed out on typewriter

23 Kiesler is here referring to the photograph of the Bordeaux bottle used by Duchamp for the production of the photomontage on the front cover of *View.*

24 *he added,* deleted in pencil.

25 This is the original position in the typescript of the two sentences "Both of us agreed ..." and "I have just bought the tie, it's new", which Kiesler circled with pencil and shifted – by a pencilled arrow – to a position in front of the previous sentence.

26 Sentence beginning with *He had ...,* deleted in pencil.

27 *put it on,* x'ed out on typewriter.

28 *He grinned, the photographer,* x'ed out on typewriter.

29 *sharp,* x'ed out on typewriter.

30 *smea,* x'ed out on typewriter.

31 *asked,* x'ed out on typewriter.

32 *lines around the mouth,* x'ed out on typewriter.

33 *would be,* deleted in pencil, replaced by *was.*

34 *Marcel asked,* x'ed out on typewriter.

35 Here Kiesler uses the word *Attendanten*, his own German rendering of the English word *attendants.*

36 The words *in my coat pocket* are written twice, deleted in pencil.

37 *About 7 foot*, written twice, deleted in pencil.

38 Just over two metres.

39 *He,* x'ed out on typewriter; *on the,* x'ed out on typewriter.

40 *on the*, x'ed out on typewriter.

41 *grasped the T[able],* x'ed out on typewriter.

42 *to wipe the brown print dry, perhaps in order to …*, deleted in pencil.

43 *rolled*, x'ed out on typewriter.

44 *assistant,* x'ed out on typewriter.

45 *came*, x'ed out on typewriter.

46 Illegible deletion

47 *in*, x'ed out on typewriter.

48 *6.30,* x'ed out on typewriter.

49 *Marcel and I sat,* x'ed out on typewriter.

50 This is the original position in the typescript of the sentences: "Marcel dashed through the hallway into the [other] room, saying: 'I've got to be downtown at 7 o'clock.'", which Kiesler circled with pencil and shifted – by a pencilled arrow – to a position in front of the two previous sentences.

51 By "two of your pages" Duchamp is probably alluding to Kiesler's planned article. The editors finally allocated six pages for Kiesler's photomontage. Duchamp can hardly have been referring to this, as the printing of small photographs on the edge of a page would have had too negative an effect on the composition of the photomontage. Moreover, Kiesler did not receive the necessary photographic prints for the production of the photomontage in the centre of the magazine until he visited the photographer's studio on January 13.

52 *The one of,* x'ed out on typewriter.

53 *I looked at the print once again,* deleted in pencil.

54 *and said,* x'ed out on typewriter.

55 Based on the elapsed time of three weeks, this visit must have taken place in the last week of December 1944, immediately after Duchamp's and Kiesler's meeting with the editors of *View* on December 22, 1944. Documentary evidence of this "check" may possibly be Kiesler's biographical notes on Duchamp, which are kept in the archive of the Austrian Frederick and Lillian Kiesler Private Foundation, Vienna, as their style of writing is similar to that of interview notes. In the *View* issue of December 1944 (no. 4, Series IV, p. 8) the editors had announced that the "special number" on Marcel Duchamp, due for publication in March, would contain "the first complete survey of his life and work". As Kiesler's notes on Duchamp's biography go far beyond the facts that were known at that time, it is certainly not unthinkable that he obtained these particulars in his interview with Duchamp with the specific aim of contributing something to the "completeness" of the survey of Duchamp's life and work. What form this contribution was to take has remained unknown to this day. A typographical version of the notes has been published in: Kraus, Sonzogni: "Wanted: Original Manuscript on Marcel Duchamp", 2003, in: http://www.toutfait.com/issues/volume2/issue_5/collections/kiesler/kiesler.html

56 *which you had meticulously scraped together with both your hands,* deleted in pencil.

57 *The mound of dust,* x'ed out on typewriter.

58 *You then showed me,* x'ed out on typewriter.

59 *was needed for coating the bottle,* deleted in pencil.

60 Kiesler had made a photomontage of Duchamp's studio at 210 W 14 St and written the title "Poème espace dédie à H(ieronymus) Duchamp" directly on the montage. It was published in the Marcel Duchamp Number of *View*, no. 1, 1945, p. 27.